SINGER

SEWING REFERENCE LIBRARY®

Sewing for Children

Cy DeCosse Incorporated
Minnetonka, Minnesota

SINGER

SEWING REFERENCE LIBRARY®

Sewing for Children

Contents

How to Use This Book 7

Copyright © 1988
Cy DeCosse Incorporated
5900 Green Oak Drive
Minnetonka, Minnesota 55343
1-800-328-3895
All rights reserved.
Printed in U.S.A.

Also available from the publisher: *Sewing
Essentials, Sewing for the Home, Clothing Care
& Repair, Sewing for Style, Sewing Specialty
Fabrics, Sewing Activewear, The Perfect Fit,
Timesaving Sewing, More Sewing for the Home,
Sewing Update, Tailoring, Sewing with an
Overlock, 101 Sewing Secrets, Sewing Pants
That Fit, Quilting by Machine, Decorative*

*Machine Stitching, Creative Sewing Ideas,
Sewing Lingerie, Sewing Projects for the Home*

Library of Congress
Cataloging-in-Publication Data

Sewing for children.

(Singer sewing reference library)
Includes index.
1. Machine sewing. 2. Children's clothing.
I. Series.
TT713.S38   1988   646.4'06   88-23701
ISBN 0-86573-243-4
ISBN 0-86573-244-2 (pbk.)

Distributed by: Contemporary Books, Inc.
Chicago, Illinois

CY DE COSSE INCORPORATED
Chairman: Cy DeCosse
President: James B. Maus
Executive Vice President: William B. Jones

SEWING FOR CHILDREN
Created by: The Editors of Cy DeCosse
Incorporated, in cooperation with the
Singer Education Department. Singer is
a trademark of the Singer Company and
is used under license.

Project Director: Rita Opseth
Project Manager: Melissa Erickson
Senior Editor: Carol Neumann

Art Director: Lisa Rosenthal
Writer: Lynn Madsen
Editors: Janice Cauley, Bernice Maehren,
  Susan Meyers
Sample Supervisors: Wendy Fedie,
  Joanne Wawra
Sewing Staff: Phyllis Galbraith, Bridget
  Haugh, Carol Neumann, Joan Coop, Cindy
  Curtis, Sheila Duffy, Mary Gannon, Judy
  Peterson, Linda Powell, Valerie Ruthardt,
  Nancy Sundeen, Barbara Vik, Mary Wagner
Fabric Editor: Marie Castle
Technical Photo Director: Bridget Haugh
Photo Studio Manager: Cathleen Shannon
Photographers: Rex Irmen, Tony Kubat, John
  Lauenstein, Mark Macemon, Mette Nielsen,
  Allen Beaulieu, Charles Nields

Production Manager: Jim Bindas
Assistant Production Managers: Julie Churchill,
  Jacquie Marx
Production Staff: Russ Beaver, Janice Cauley,
  Holly Clements, Sheila DiPaola, Joe Fahey,
  Carol Ann Kevan, Yelena Konrardy, Robert
  Lynch, Cindy Natvig, Dave Schelitzche,
  Linda Schloegel, Jennie Smith, Greg
  Wallace, Nik Wogstad
Consultants: Kitty Benton, Virginia Carney,
  Jana Davis, Zoe Graul, Vicki Hastings, Carol
  Jones, Jackie Kanthak, JoAnn Krause,
  Christine Nelson, Melanie Nelson-Smith,
  Barbara Palmer, Kathy Sandmann, Mary
  Pat Sweetman
Contributing Manufacturers: B. Blumenthal
  & Co., Inc.; Butterick Company, Inc.;

Clotilde; Coats & Clark; Daisy Kingdom,
Inc; Dritz Corporation; Dyno
Merchandise Corporation; EZ
International; Freudenberg, Pellon
Division; June Tailor, Inc.; Kwik Sew
Pattern Company; The McCall Pattern
Company; Minnetonka Mills, Inc.; Olfa
Products Corporation; Rowenta, Inc.; Sew
Easy Textiles, Inc.; Simplicity Pattern
Company, Inc; The Singer Company;
Speed Stitch, Inc.; Stacy Industries, Inc.;
Stretch & Sew, Inc.; Sunrise Industries,
Inc.; Swiss-Metrosene, Inc.; Vin Max, Inc.;
YKK Home Sewing Division
Color Separations: Spectrum, Inc.
Printing: Ringier America, Inc. (1291)

How to Use This Book

Sewing for Children will help you sew customized, professional-quality children's garments easily and quickly. Use this book to plan and sew attractive clothing and accessories for infants, toddlers, and school-age children. Garments should be comfortable, durable, and becoming to the child.

Sewing for Children contains complete and detailed instructions for some projects; for others, it gives helpful hints and creative ideas.

Most children's clothing has less detail than adult clothing and can be sewn in a shorter period of time. Many of the projects in this book are excellent starting points for the novice sewer or for someone who has not sewn for a number of years. Experienced sewers will find helpful shortcuts and suggestions for pattern variations or adaptations.

To make the most efficient use of your time, become familiar with information in the Getting Started section of the book before you select a project. Learn about up-to-date equipment, notions, fabrics, patterns, and styles. Sewing techniques for the serger, or overlock machine, are included where appropriate. When a serging method is shown, a conventional sewing machine method is also suggested.

Directions for specific methods are given step-by-step, with close-up photographs for explicit detail. In some photographs, contrasting thread is used to highlight the sewing technique, but you will want to use matching thread for your own projects, unless contrasting thread is desired for a decorative effect.

Sewing for Children's Changing Needs

Making clothing for children is different from sewing for adults. Although children's clothing requires less fitting, children grow quickly and have different clothing needs at different ages. Use the Infants section for planning a layette and gathering decorating ideas for the nursery. You may also want to choose specific projects, ranging from bedding and bibs to kimonos and kimono variations.

The Growing Up section of the book covers activewear for toddlers and children. Included are tips for adding durability and room for growth to garments you sew. You will also find many creative ideas for making a garment special. To get the most versatility and use from garments you sew for a child, follow the wardrobe planning tips to coordinate garments. As children begin dressing themselves and selecting their own clothes, they often express strong preferences; you may want to involve the child in the planning when choosing colors, styles, and fabrics.

Using Your Creativity

Some of the ideas in this book are as simple as using a unique notion or closure. In the Personalizing section, we have included several techniques for adding a personal touch to a garment by sewing a patchwork border, mixing fabrics creatively, or using the artistic ideas of the child who will wear the garment. Many of these personalizing techniques are not limited to the garments that you sew, but can also be used to customize T-shirts and other purchased clothing. With the help of *Sewing for Children,* you can sew more creatively by customizing children's clothing.

The Dressing Up section of the book introduces several types of dresswear. Some projects are simple, creative additions or adjustments to a garment. This section also helps you achieve a hand-sewn heirloom look, using up-to-date techniques on the sewing machine. With machine heirloom techniques you can make a christening dress or other special garment that may be treasured for generations.

Choosing Children's Clothing

Sewing children's clothes can be quite economical and need not be time-consuming. Because children's garments require less fabric than garments for adults, the fabric cost is usually minimal. You may be able to use fabric from other sewing projects to construct a garment, or part of a garment, for a young child.

Most children's clothing designs follow simple lines, have few pieces, and are easy to sew. They are a good starting point for a beginning sewer or for a sewer whose skills need updating.

Planning for Safety

Build safety into children's garments. Avoid loose strings or excess fabric that may get tangled, especially for infants. Beware of long skirts or gowns that may cause a child to trip, or very full sleeves that may catch on objects. Limit tie belts and drawstrings to short lengths, and securely fasten buttons and trims. Use fire-retardant fabrics for sleepwear.

Customizing Clothes for Children

Creative touches can make a garment special to a child. Use a child's crayon drawing as a guide to colors and shapes for a machine-embroidered design. Or let children color or paint fabric before you cut out the pattern. Some children may enjoy designing their clothes by drawing the garment they would like and then having you match the color and general style. Simple, original appliqués can reflect a favorite hobby or special toy.

Involve the child in selecting patterns, fabrics, and notions. For young children learning to identify colors, primary colors of red, yellow, and blue are popular. Look at colors of a favorite toy and the colors a child often chooses for painting or drawing. Consider the coloring of the child's hair, eyes, and skin; select colors that compliment them.

Features for Self-dressing

To encourage self-dressing, choose garments with loose-fitting necklines and waistlines and with manageable fasteners. Make closures easy to see and reach on the front or side of a garment. Hook and loop tape can be used for closures on most types of garments. Young children can easily unfasten simple, large, round buttons and snaps, but may have difficulty closing them with small hands. They also enjoy smooth-running zippers with large teeth and zipper pulls. Pull-on pants that have elastic waists are easier for young children to pull on and off. Children can be frustrated by trying to fasten hooks and eyes, tiny buttons, and ties.

Tips for Planning Garments for Growth and Comfort

Add ribbing cuffs to lower edges of sleeves or pants legs so you can turn up built-in room for growth.

Choose pants patterns in a style that can be cut off for shorts when outgrown in length.

Use elastic waists on generously sized pants or skirts for comfort during growth spurts.

Allow extra crotch and body length in one-piece garments to prevent them from becoming uncomfortable as the child grows.

Add elastic suspenders with adjustable closures.

Choose dress and jumper patterns with dropped waist or no waist for comfort and maximum length of wear.

Use knit fabrics for easier sewing and maximum stretch for growth and comfort.

Consider patterns with pleats, gathers, and wide shapes that allow for growth without riding up.

Select patterns with raglan, dolman, and dropped sleeves to offer room for growth and less restriction of movement.

Select oversized styles for comfort.

Selecting Patterns

All children are comfortable in loose-fitting garments, but their clothing requirements change as they grow. For infants, select one-piece garments, such as kimonos, that make it easy to dress the baby and change the diapers. Toddlers are also comfortable in one-piece garments, such as overalls, with a crotch opening. Two-piece styles with elastic waistbands are easy to get on and off and are practical for children who are being toilet-trained. Adjustable shoulder straps and straps that crisscross at the back, as well as elastic waistbands, help keep pants and skirts in place.

Look for basic, versatile styles. Coordinated pants, shirts, skirts, jackets, overalls, and sweatsuits can be worn year-round. Except for skirts, these garments can be worn by both boys and girls. Use a basic pattern to plan a mix-and-match wardrobe. Coordinate fabrics and notions, and save time by sewing several garments, using the same pattern.

Selecting a Pattern Size

Buy patterns according to the child's measurements, not the child's age or ready-to-wear size. Compare the child's measurements with the chart on the pattern or in a pattern catalog. Most pattern measurement charts are standardized; however, the fit of similar garments may vary, even though the same size pattern is used. The style of the garment, whether it is loose-fitting or close-fitting, and the amount of ease added for movement and comfort affect the fit.

You may want to compare the pattern with a well-fitting garment to check the fit of the garment you intend to make. If the child is between two sizes, buy the larger size pattern. Multi-sized patterns can be used for several sizes. To preserve the original pattern, trace each size as it is used.

To reflect the changing shape of growing bodies, pattern sizes for different ages use different body measurements. Infants' patterns give the baby's length and weight. Toddlers' patterns give chest, waist, and approximate height measurements. The Toddlers' sizes are shorter in length than Children's sizes and have extra room for diapers. Children's sizes give measurements for chest, waist, hip, and approximate height. Up to a size 6, Children's patterns generally increase one size for each additional inch (2.5 cm) around the body.

Fitting

Most children's garments require minimal fitting. Even if some of the child's measurements differ slightly from those on the pattern, you may not need to make adjustments. For example, a garment with elastic at the waist may not need a waistline adjustment. Determine adjustments before cutting the fabric. Make the same amount of adjustment to adjoining pattern pieces, and preserve the grainline on the adjusted pattern. You can make some adjustments as you sew by using wider or narrower seam allowances.

Adjusting Pattern Length and Width

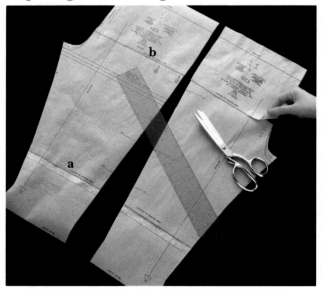

Lengthen (a) or shorten (b) pattern at adjustment lines. Spread or lap pattern pieces to desired adjustment; tape, preserving grainline. Blend the cutting and stitching lines.

Increase (a) or decrease (b) width up to ¼" (6 mm) on each side seam allowance for total adjustment up to 1" (2.5 cm). To increase or decrease width more than 1" (2.5 cm), use different pattern size. On bodices, you will need to adjust ease in sleeve to fit new armhole size.

Taking Measurements

To take a child's measurements, use a tape measure or brightly colored nonstretch ribbon held snugly, but not tightly. The child should wear underwear or diapers and stand in a natural position. For a very young or active child, you can measure a garment that fits well and compare it with the garment size on the pattern envelope. You will not need all measurements every time you sew.

Head. Measure around the fullest part of the head. This measurement is important for garments without neckline plackets.

Chest. Measure around the fullest part of the chest, just over the shoulder blades.

Waist. Toddlers often do not have a distinct waistline. To determine the natural waistline, tie a string around the midsection; have the child move and bend. The string will fall into place; measure over the string.

Hips. Measure around the fullest part of the hips.

Back waist length. Measure from the prominent bone at the neck to the natural waistline; you can locate the neckbone when the child's head is bent forward.

Arm-across-back length. With the child's arm extended straight out at the side, measure from the wrist across the shoulder to the middle of the neck. Place the sleeve pattern next to the garment back pattern, overlapping seam allowances; measure pattern from wrist to center back. You can now compare the body measurement with the pattern measurement.

Crotch depth. Tie a string around the waist. Have the child sit on a chair; measure at the side from the waist to the seat of the chair.

Finished dress or skirt length. Measure from a string at the waist to the desired hem length.

Finished pants length. Measure from a string at the waist to the anklebone.

Selecting Fabrics

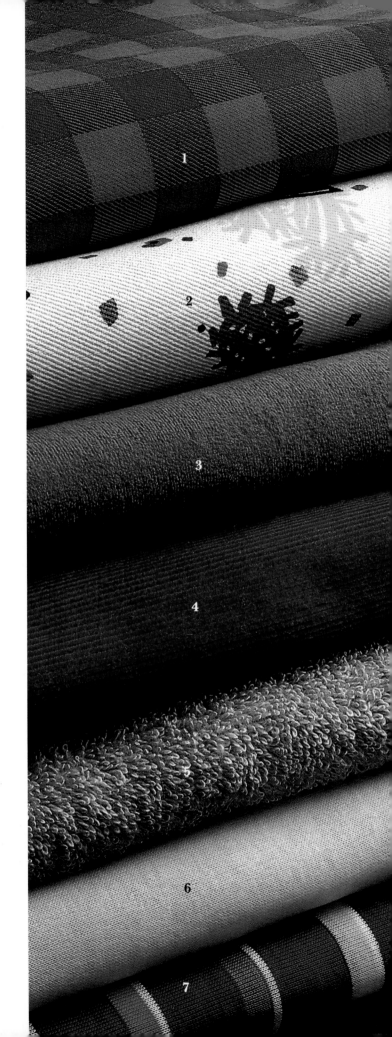

Children's everyday garments need to withstand the wear and tear of active play and numerous launderings. For these clothes, select durable, comfortable, easy-care fabrics. For special-occasion clothing, use velvets, velveteens, and taffetas. For heirloom sewing, look for even-weave fabrics that are fine, soft, and drapable; they may be sheer, and with or without sheen. Although 100 percent cotton is durable and consistent with the look of antique garments, it does require ironing. The easy-care features of polyester/cotton blends appeal to some sewers. Use sheer fabrics, such as polyester/cotton Imperial® batiste and 100 percent cotton Swiss batiste.

Natural fibers are soft and nonabrasive. They offer breathability and moisture absorption, qualities lacking in pure synthetics; but natural fibers may require more care. Synthetic fibers, such as acrylic and polyester, are easy-care, but they do not breathe or absorb moisture. They stain easily, and with repeated launderings they eventually pill, yellow, and lose their softness. Blends of natural and synthetic fibers combine the best properties of each to produce soft, absorbent, wrinkle-free fabrics.

Fabric Types

Woven fabrics that are sheer and lightweight are suitable for blouses, shirts, dresses, and skirts. Firmly woven fabrics are most durable; choose them for pants, shirts, and jackets. Woven fabrics best suited for sewing children's clothing are: batiste, broadcloth, calico, chambray, chino, cotton Swiss batiste, denim, dotted Swiss, duck, gingham, madras, organdy, polyester/cotton Imperial batiste, polyester taffeta, poplin, sailcloth, seersucker, shirting, twill, and voile.

Knit fabrics are a good choice, because children are active and knits give as the body moves. When selecting knits, check the stretch of the fabric with the gauge on the pattern envelope. Knit fabrics include: cotton spandex, double knit, interlock, jersey, sweatshirt fleece, and thermal knit.

Fabrics with nap have a surface texture that feels soft or brushed, and may be either woven or knit. These fabrics include: brushed denim, corduroy, double-faced polyester bunting, flannel, French terry, piqué, stretch terry, terry cloth, velvet, velveteen, and velour.

Fabrics for children's clothing include: shirting (**1**), denim (**2**), velour (**3**), corduroy (**4**), terry cloth (**5**), interlock (**6**), jersey (**7**), dotted Swiss (**8**), Imperial batiste (**9**), taffeta (**10**).

Specialty Trims

The finest specialty trims are 100 percent cotton or a blend with a high proportion of cotton. They feature a fine weave, and the designs are cleanly finished. Both edges of lace insertion (1) are straight. Lace edgings (2) have one straight edge and one scalloped edge.

Lace beading (3) has holes for threading ribbon. Eyelets and embroideries (4) may be embroidered in white or a color and are available as insertions, edgings, or beading. Entredeux (5) is used to separate trims and fabric and has seam allowances on both sides.

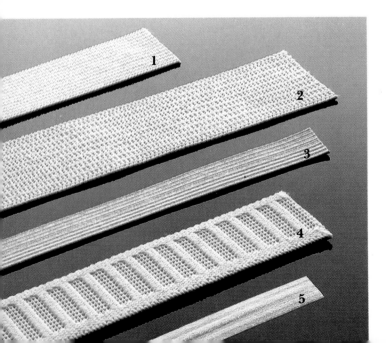

Elastic

Elastics vary in stretch and recovery characteristics. Look for elastics that retain their original width when stretched and that recover to their original length when applied to a garment. Those made from cotton and rubber are the most durable.

Knitted (1) and woven (2) elastics are most appropriate for stitching directly to the garment. Braided (3) and nonroll (4) elastic are suitable for casings. Transparent (5) elastic blends with any fabric color and is comfortable next to the skin.

Ribbing

The stretch and recovery of ribbing varies widely. The stretch is acceptable if a 4" (10 cm) piece stretches fully to about 7" (18 cm).

The finished width of ribbing is in proportion to the garment edge and size. Cut the ribbing twice the finished width plus ½" (1.3 cm) for two ¼" (6 mm) seam allowances. Trim the garment seam allowances to ¼" (6 mm) on edges where ribbing will be applied. Use the method below to cut ribbing to fit the edge of the garment. Or, for a closer fit at wrist, waistline, and pants leg, cut the ribbing to fit the body. It may then be necessary to gather the garment edge to fit the ribbing.

Tubular ribbing is 18" to 22" (46 to 56 cm) wide and is sold by the inch (2.5 cm). It is available in two weights. The lighter weight is suitable for use on T-shirt knits, sweatshirt fleece, velours, and lightweight woven fabrics. The heavier weight is used for outerwear or heavyweight fabrics. Do not preshrink ribbing; this distorts the ribbing and makes accurate layout and cutting difficult.

Guide to Cut Width of Ribbings (includes seam allowances)

Garment Edge	Infants'	Toddlers'	Children's
Short sleeve	2" (5 cm)	2½" (6.5 cm)	2½" (6.5 cm)
Standard crew neck	2½" (6.5 cm)	2½" (6.5 cm)	3" (7.5 cm)
Narrow crew neck	2" (5 cm)	2" (5 cm)	2½" (6.5 cm)
Prefinished collar	2½" (6.5 cm)	2¾" (7 cm)	3" (7.5 cm)
Waistband, wrists, pants legs	4¼" (10.8 cm)	5" (12.5 cm)	6½" (16.3 cm)
Pocket	2" (5 cm)	2" (5 cm)	2½" (6.5 cm)

How to Measure and Cut Ribbing

1) **Measure** pattern edge where ribbing is to be applied, standing tape measure on edge at seamline. For neck and waist edges, double this measurement.

2) **Cut** ribbing two-thirds the measured length of seamline and twice desired finished width; add ½" (1.3 cm) to length and width for seam allowances.

Equipment & Tools

A basic conventional sewing machine with a zigzag stitch works well for sewing children's clothing, although a computerized sewing machine can be helpful for adding embellishments. For small, hard-to-reach areas, such as knees and elbows, a free-arm sewing machine is useful. A serger, or overlock machine, does not replace a conventional machine, but it can cut sewing time considerably; it sews a seam at the same time it finishes and trims the edges.

Sewing machine accessories help make sewing for children more efficient. The ruffler attachment (1) saves time when you are sewing numerous ruffles or pleats. The pin-tuck foot (2) is used with twin needles (3) for making tucks of various sizes. Twin needles also work well for reinforcement stitches and hems. A general-purpose presser foot (4) and needle plate (5) are used with wing needles (6), which create holes in fabric to produce a decorative effect.

Ballpoint needles are used for sewing knits. Universal point needles are designed to

be used with knits and woven fabrics. A fine needle, size 9 (65), is used for fine, lightweight fabrics.

A bodkin (7) is a long metal or plastic tool that is handy for threading elastic, ribbon, and cord through a casing. A rotary cutter (8) is available in two sizes and comes with a retractable blade for safety. The large rotary cutter quickly cuts several layers at a time and can be used for heavy fabrics. The small rotary cutter is used for single thicknesses, lightweight fabrics, and small curves. Use a rotary cutter with a cutting mat (9). Fastener pliers (10) are used for installing fasteners such as gripper snaps and eyelets.

A puff iron (11) is convenient to use when you are making machine heirloom clothing. It uses dry heat and irons delicate fabrics without scorching. A sleeve board is versatile for use in narrow seam areas, such as sleeves and pants legs.

Notions

You may want to stockpile assorted notions to make it easy to vary garments made from a single pattern.

Closures on children's garments may be decorative as well as functional. Snaps come in a variety of weights and colors. Novelty buttons add a special detail, but small or shaped buttons can make it difficult for young children to dress themselves. Hook and loop tape is an easier fastener for children to manage.

Zippers may also be decorative, especially when used in contrasting colors. Zippers with fine coils are available for use on small garments. Zipper coil, with separate zipper pulls, is available in rolls of 5½ yd. (5.05 m) or by the inch (2.5 cm). It allows you to make zippers of any length and eliminates the need for keeping various sizes of zippers on hand. Dye the zipper and zipper pull to match garments or to coordinate with them.

Hardware such as D-rings, snap hooks, plastic sliders, and overall buckles can be used for suspenders, belts, and adjustable straps. Tapes and trims include ribbons, bias and twill tapes, piping, and braid. Reflective tape can be applied as a safety measure to clothing worn outdoors after dark. Appliqués add a custom look.

Getting Ready to Sew

It is important to preshrink washable fabrics, trims, and notions before laying out patterns. Preshrinking prevents the garment from shrinking, and seams and trims from puckering. It also removes excess dye and chemical finishes. Do not preshrink ribbing; this distorts the ribbing and makes accurate layout and cutting difficult.

Preshrink and dry washable fabrics as recommended in the fabric care instructions. After preshrinking 100 percent cotton fabrics, it is important to launder them several times before cutting, because cotton fabrics continue to shrink during the first several launderings. Preshrink dark and vivid cottons separately, until colors are stabilized. To preshrink fabrics that require drycleaning, steam them evenly with a steam iron and allow them to dry thoroughly on a smooth, flat surface.

Some knits, especially lightweight cotton knits, may curl and ripple after preshrinking. Remove wrinkles from the fabric before laying out the pattern, making sure the lengthwise grain is straight. Press pattern pieces with a warm, dry iron.

Plaid, striped, and checked fabrics add variety to children's garments. When using one of these fabrics, select a pattern with few pieces to make it easier to match the design. Stand back and look at the fabric to determine the dominant part of the design. The easiest way to cut these fabrics is as a single layer. Cut out each pattern piece from the fabric, and turn the cut fabric piece over to use as a pattern so the design on the second piece will match the first piece.

Tips for Laying Out Plaid Fabrics

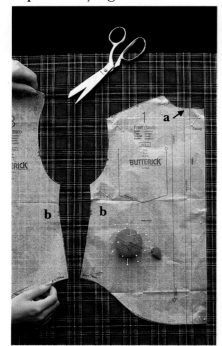

Lay out each piece in a single layer, beginning with front pattern piece. Use dominant part of design (**a**) for center front and center back. Match notches at side seams (**b**) of front and back.

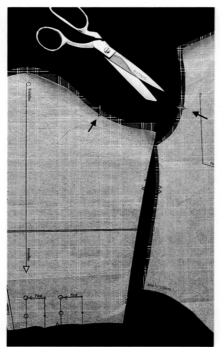

Center sleeve at same dominant part of design as center front. The design should match at the notches (arrows) of the sleeve front and armhole of garment front; notches at back may not match.

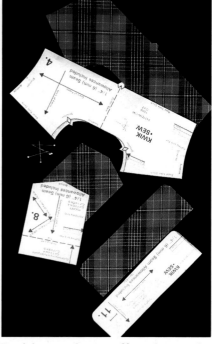

Position pockets, cuffs, yokes, and separate front bands on true bias to avoid time-consuming matching. Center a dominant design block in each pattern piece.

Tips for Layout, Cutting, and Marking

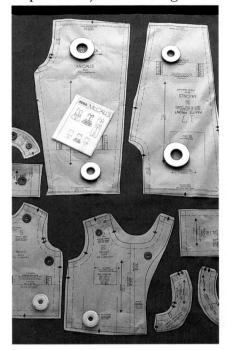

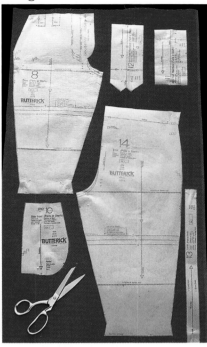

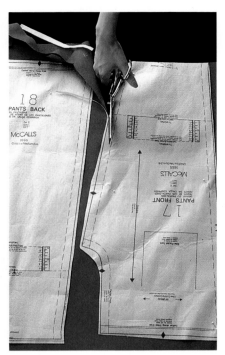

Refer to pattern layout diagram on guidesheet. Position pattern pieces, following grainline arrows and nap direction. Use weights to hold the pattern in place.

Lay out all pattern pieces on napped fabric with upper edge of pattern pieces toward same end of fabric. Corduroy and other napped fabrics wear better if sewn with the nap running down garment.

Use sharp shears and long strokes for smooth cutting. Do not trim excess pattern tissue before cutting fabric unless cutting thick fabrics such as corduroy and quilted fabric.

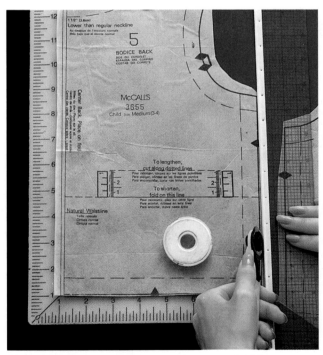

Use rotary cutter with protective mat, shifting mat to cut other pieces. Use metal-edged ruler for straight edges, placing blade side of rotary cutter next to ruler; trim off notches. Small rotary cutter may be used for tight curves or complex shapes.

Transfer all pattern markings after cutting. Make short clip no more than ⅛" (3 mm) into seam allowance to mark notches, dots, center front, center back, and ends of darts and pleats. To mark pockets, pin through pattern and fabric, lift pattern, and mark each fabric layer with chalk or washable marking pen.

Timesaving Techniques

You can save time by planning your sewing carefully. Use the same pattern to make several of the garments most commonly worn by the child, and purchase fabrics that can be sewn with the same thread color or invisible thread. If you plan coordinating colors, you can achieve a custom look by interchanging cuff and trim pieces among several garments.

Eliminating center front and center back seams saves cutting and construction time. Another timesaving technique is to select a pattern that has ¼" (6 mm) seam allowances, or trim the pattern seam allowances to ¼" (6 mm) as you cut. You can also save time by using weights instead of pins to hold fabric in place. Glue-stick or water-soluble basting glue can be used in place of pins and hand basting.

Stack three or four light to mediumweight fabrics of the same width to cut at one time. Cut front and back pieces on folds; do not cut any center front openings at this time. Use rotary cutter with guide arm to trim seam allowances to ¼" (6 mm) while cutting out garment.

Determine which garments will have ribbings, elastic, front openings, or trims. Cut ribbings and trims to correct size. Group the fabric for each garment with the corresponding notions and trims.

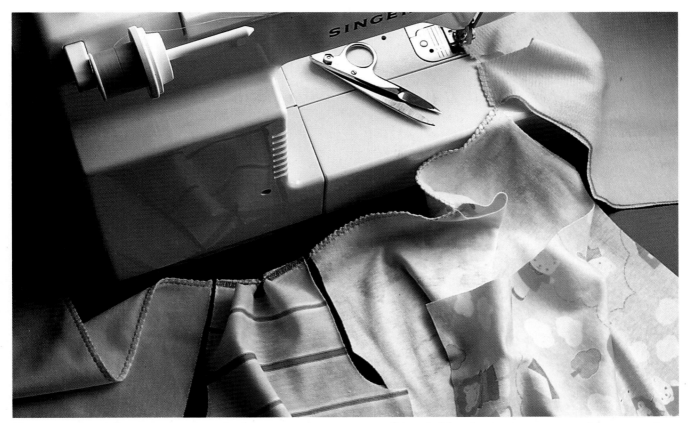

Group garments that use same thread color, so you can sew all at one time. Use continuous stitching wherever possible, stitching from seam to seam without stopping. Cut threads after all garments are stitched.

Organize work sessions according to type of activity. Do all straight-stitching at one time, as well as all pressing, seam finishing, and zigzagging or serging. Attach closures at end of sewing process.

Hems & Seams

Topstitched hems and seams can be decorative as well as functional. Use a matching or contrasting color thread that coordinates with other items of clothing.

Machine-stitched hems are fast and durable, and are a good alternative for ribbing at cuffs, waistlines, and pants legs on children's clothing.

Select seams and seam finishes based on the type of fabric. Also consider if the seam will show through the garment, if strength is required at the seam, and if the seam will be comfortable when it is next to the skin.

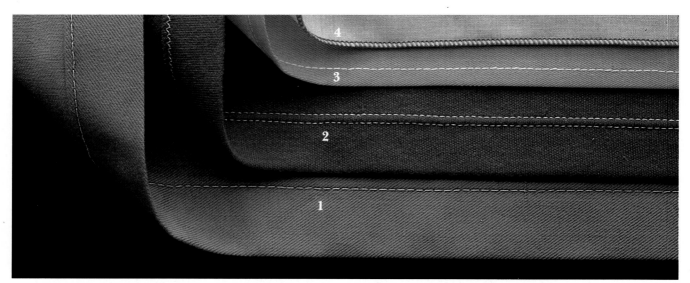

Hems. Topstitched hem (1) has one or more rows of topstitching near upper edge of a finished hem allowance. A twin-needle topstitched hem (2) is suitable for knits, because the bobbin thread zigzags on the wrong side and allows stitches to stretch. Stitch about ¼" (6 mm) below cut edge of hem allowance and trim close to stitching. For a narrow hem (3), trim hem allowance to ½" (1.3 cm); press to wrong side. Open hem, and fold raw edge to hemline crease. Fold again to make double-fold hem; topstitch one or two rows as desired. Use a rolled hem (4), sewn on a serger, for lightweight or sheer fabrics. Stitch with right side up; fabric rolls under to the wrong side.

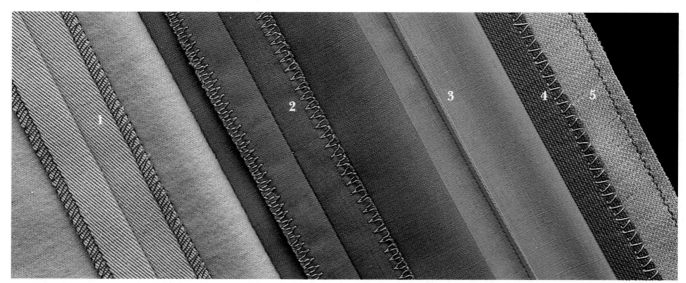

Seams and seam finishes. For plain seams, press open ⅝" (1.5 cm) seam allowances. Finish edges with overlock stitching (1) sewn on a serger, or with a three-step zigzag (2). A French seam (3) is neat and inconspicuous from the right side, but it is difficult to use on curves. For ¼" (6 mm) seam allowances on stretch fabrics, use an overedge stitch (4) or a narrow zigzag stitch (5); stretch seams slightly while stitching. Press narrow seams to one side.

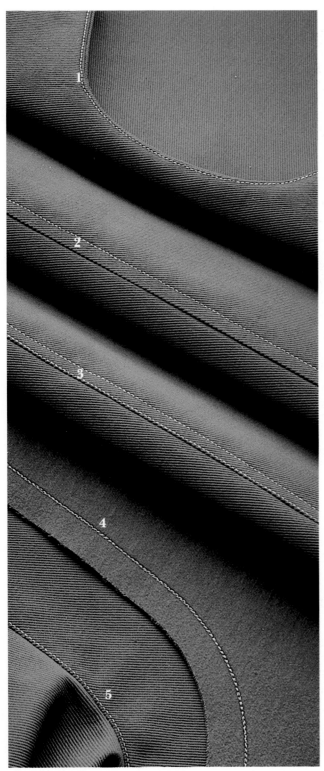

Reinforced seams. Understitched seam (**1**) stabilizes the seam by stitching seam allowances to the facing. Welt seam (**2**) has seam allowances pressed to one side and topstitched to garment. Mock flat-fell seam (**3**) has exposed seam allowances on the wrong side of the garment with topstitching and edgestitching. Double-stitching (**4**) is stitching sewn over previous stitching. Edgestitching (**5**) is stitching sewn on the right side of the garment, through both seam allowances, as close to the seamline as possible.

Overlock seams. 3-thread stitch (**1**) stretches with the fabric and can be used as a seam or edge finish, but it is not recommended for woven fabrics in areas of stress. 4-thread stitch with chainstitch (**2**) is strong and stable for woven fabrics, but it does not stretch on knit seams. 4/3-thread stitch (**3**) provides an additional line of stitching, has stretch, and can be used on knit fabrics. Flatlock seam (**4**) is less bulky and lies flat.

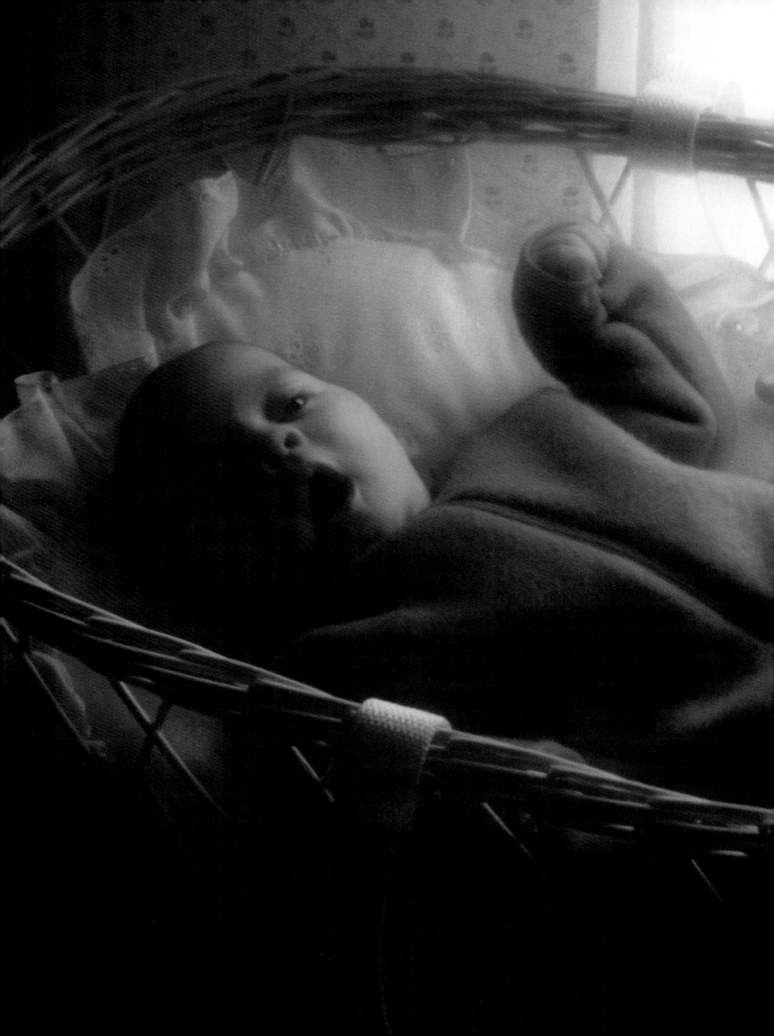

Infants

Sewing a Basic Layette

Many of the items in a basic layette, such as receiving blankets, hooded towels, bibs, kimonos, and buntings, are easy and practical to sew. Multi-sized layette patterns are available for making most of these items. For everyday wear, use simple, loose-fitting designs and high-quality fabrics that are easy to sew and launder.

Cotton or cotton-blend fabrics are good choices because cotton breathes, absorbs moisture, and is easy to launder. Infants are most comfortable in soft fabrics.

Stretch knits adapt well to movement, growth, and easy dressing. Woven fabrics such as flannel, seersucker, and broadcloth work well with the addition of ribbing at the neck, sleeves, and hem.

Federal regulations require that garments designed for children's sleepwear meet flame-retardancy standards. Look for this information on the ends of fabric bolts. Cotton must be blended with synthetic fibers to accept this treatment.

If you select basic styles, you can use timesaving techniques that allow you to sew several garments in a short time. By choosing high-quality fabrics, you

can sew garments superior to the average ready-to-wear items, and often at a more reasonable cost.

Receiving blankets and hooded towels are important to a layette. Several blankets or towels can be made at a time. Hooded towels can also be used as beach towels.

Bibs can easily be made by sewing ribbing and a neck closure to a hand towel. Older infants and toddlers enjoy large bibs with sleeves and pockets, which you can coordinate with several garments.

Kimonos of soft flannel or knits are comfortable for an infant during the first several months, and the open lower edge of the kimono allows for easy diapering. If the neck and armhole openings are large enough, the garment can also be used as a dress or T-shirt in later months. Buntings, adaptations of the kimono, are closed at the lower edge for outerwear use and are often made of quilted fabrics, double-faced polyester bunting, or other soft, heavyweight fabrics.

Infant Accessories

Patterns are available for infant seat covers, pillows, diaper stackers, high chair pads, and other accessories. All of these can be customized by using coordinating colors, extra padding, warm fabrics, ruffles, and piping. Patterns may need to be adapted to the specific needs of the equipment; for example, tie and strap locations may need to be adjusted.

Receiving Blankets & Hooded Towels

Receiving blankets and hooded towels can be made large enough to accommodate the growth of the child. Choose soft, warm, and absorbent woven or knit fabrics. Select from flannel, interlock, jersey, thermal knit, terry cloth and stretch terry. Two layers of lightweight fabric can be used with wrong sides together. Round all corners for easy edge application.

Cut a 36" (91.5 cm) square blanket or towel from 1 yd. (.95 m) of 45" or 60" (115 or 152.5 cm) wide fabric. When using 45" (115 cm) wide fabric, the mock binding and hood require an additional ¼ yd. (.25 m). Cut a 1½" (3.8 cm) wide binding strip on the lengthwise or crosswise grain, 2" (5 cm) longer than the distance around the item; piece, as necessary. Press binding in half, with wrong sides together.

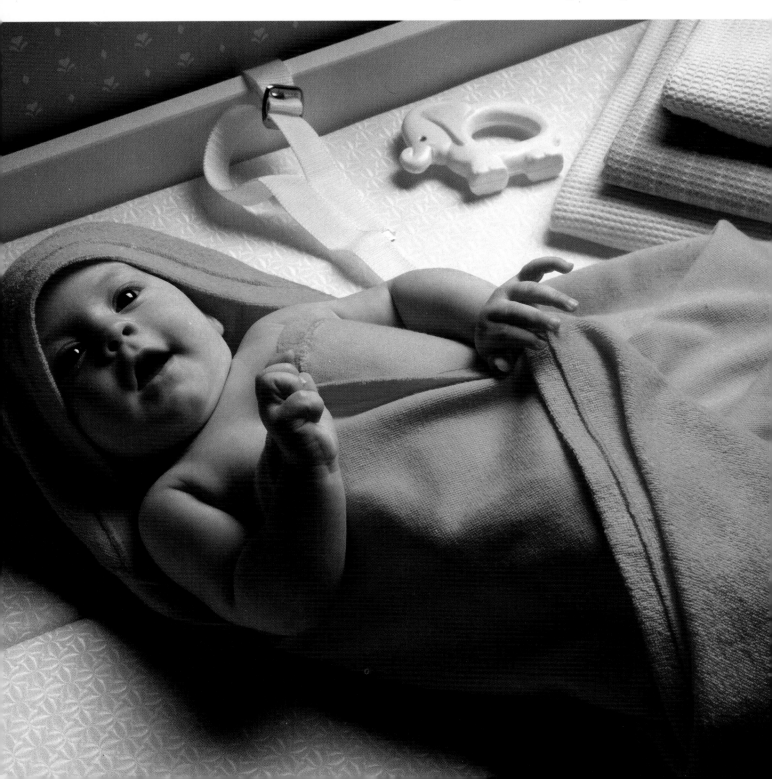

How to Finish Edges with a Mock Binding

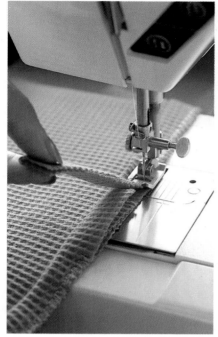

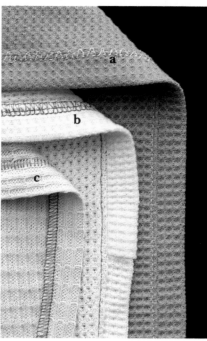

1) Use overedge stitch or serge binding to right side of fabric, starting 1½" (3.8 cm) from end of binding. Stitch to within 2" (5 cm) of start of binding, stretching fabric slightly at corners; do not stretch binding. (If flatlock stitch on serger is used, stitch *wrong* sides together.)

2) Fold 1" (2.5 cm) of binding to inside; lap around first end of binding. Continue stitching binding to fabric, stitching over previous stitches for 1" (2.5 cm) to secure the ends.

3) Turn seam allowance toward blanket or towel; topstitch through all layers of overedged **(a)** or serged **(b)** seam, to hold seam allowances flat. If flatlock **(c)** stitch is used, pull binding and fabric flat.

How to Sew a Hooded Towel

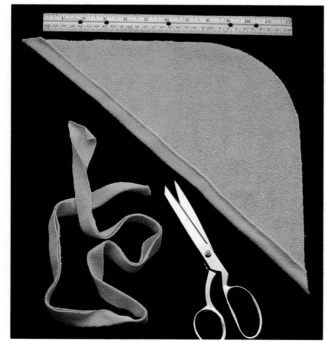

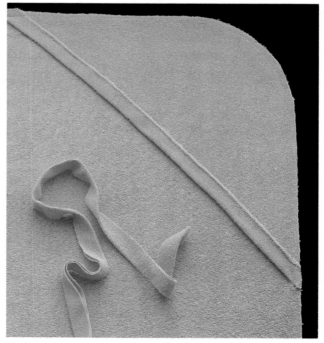

1) Cut a right triangle with two 12" (30.5 cm) sides from matching or contrasting fabric. Round right angle corner, and finish diagonal edge with mock binding, above.

2) Position wrong side of the hood to right side of the towel. Stitch triangle to one rounded corner of towel, ¼" (6 mm) from matched edges. Finish outside edges, above.

Bibs

Infant bibs are quick and easy to make. Create durable bibs from terry cloth or knit fabric or from fingertip towels, and customize the bibs with simple appliqué techniques and bias tape. Increase absorbency by using a double layer of fabric. Back a fabric bib with soft, pliable plastic to protect clothing; finish edges with wide double-fold bias tape. Or use a fingertip towel with prefinished edges.

Custom Bibs

Attach a toy or pacifier to a bib with a snap-on strip (**1**). Stitch together the edges of a 12" (30.5 cm) strip of wide double-fold bias tape, and fold under the ends of the strip. Attach one end to the bib with the ball half of a gripper snap. Attach the socket half of the gripper snap to the other end of the tape. Slip the toy or pacifier onto the tape; snap securely to the bib.

A purchased squeaker can be inserted between the appliqué and bib (**2**) before you stitch the appliqué (page 91).

A fingertip towel makes an absorbent, washable bib. Fold the towel for double absorbency under the chin (**3**), and attach double-fold bias tape around the neck edge.

How to Make a Pullover Bib

1) Use fingertip towel. Cut 5" (12.5 cm) circle with center of circle one-third the distance from one end of towel. Cut 3" (7.5 cm) wide ribbing, with length two-thirds the circumference. Stitch short ends to form circle, using ¼" (6 mm) seam allowance.

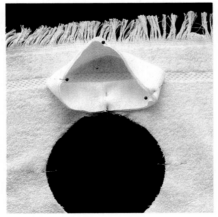

2) Fold ribbing in half, with wrong sides together. Divide ribbing and neck edge into fourths; pin-mark. Matching pins, and with seam at center back, pin ribbing to neck edge, with raw edges even. Stitch ¼" (6 mm) seam, stretching ribbing to fit neckline.

3) Fold seam allowance toward bib. Edgestitch to bib through all layers.

How to Make a Tie-on Bib

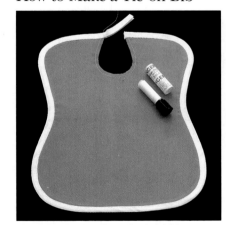

1) Press wide double-fold bias tape to follow curve of outer edge of bib. Glue-baste tape over raw edge of bib, positioning the wider tape edge on the wrong side; edgestitch in place.

2) Cut bias tape 30" (76 cm) longer than neck curve. Center bias tape over the neck edge; glue-baste. Edgestitch from one end of tie around neckline to other end. Bar tack bias tape at edge of bib (arrow) by zigzagging in place; tie knot at each end.

Alternative. Cut fingertip towel as for pullover bib, opposite. Fold so neck opening forms a half circle. Zigzag raw edges together with wide stitch. Apply bias tape for ties and neck finish, step 2, left.

Kimonos

Timesaving techniques enable you to cut and sew several kimonos at one time. Neckline openings for woven fabrics should be at least 1" to 2" (2.5 to 5 cm) larger than the infant's head. Openings for knit fabrics do not need to be as large, because knits will stretch to fit over the head.

Use the flat method of construction to sew infant-size garments; complete as much stitching as possible while the garment is flat. Access to parts of tiny garments becomes difficult once seams are completed. Apply all ribbing while one seam is still open.

How to Sew a Kimono with Ribbing (flat method)

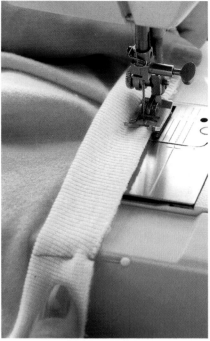

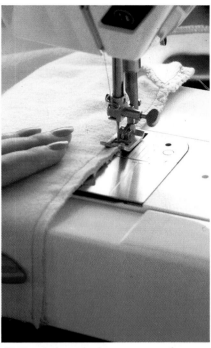

1) Measure and cut ribbing for neck, wrists, and lower edge (page 17); fold in half lengthwise. Straight-stitch or serge garment front and back together at one shoulder seam, right sides together.

2) Divide ribbing and neck edge into fourths; pin-mark. Pin the ribbing and the neck edge together at marks and ends. Overedge stitch or serge ¼" (6 mm) seam, stretching ribbing to fit neck edge as you sew.

3) Straight-stitch or serge other shoulder seam, right sides together; carefully match ribbing edge and ribbing seam. Finish the seam allowances, if necessary.

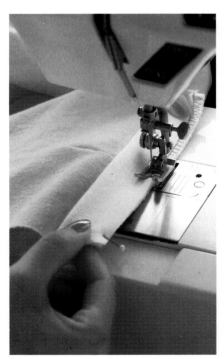

4) Divide ribbing and wrist edge in half; pin-mark. Pin and stitch as in step 2, above.

5) Straight-stitch or serge one underarm seam, with right sides together; carefully match ribbing edge and ribbing seam. Finish seam allowances, if necessary.

6) Divide ribbing and lower edge; pin and stitch as in step 2, above. Stitch remaining underarm seam as in step 5, left. Finish seam allowances, if necessary.

Customizing Kimonos

To add a placket, slash the front of the kimono and apply a continuous self-binding. Position the opening off-center so fasteners line up on the center front.

For a boy's garment, mark the placket opening to the right of center to lap left over right. For a girl's garment, mark the placket opening to the left of center to lap right over left. The photos that follow are for a girl's kimono. Mark a 6" (15 cm) opening ⅜" (1 cm) from

the center front for a ¾" (2 cm) finished placket width. Cut a binding strip 12" × 2" (30.5 × 5 cm) on the lengthwise grain. Press the binding strip in half lengthwise, wrong sides together. Open the strip, and press under ¼" (6 mm) on one long edge.

For a kimono pattern without a cuff, add sleeve mitts to be folded over the baby's hands. Finish the kimono with a mandarin collar and gripper snaps.

How to Apply a Continuous Self-bound Placket

1) Mark the placket opening, and cut binding, above. Staystitch ¼" (6 mm) from marked line, tapering to a point. Shorten stitches for ½" (1.3 cm) on each side of point, and take one short stitch at point. Slash along line to, but not through, point.

2) Hold placket opening straight; pin to unpressed edge of binding, right sides together. Stitch over staystitching with ¼" (6 mm) seam allowance on binding; raw edges match only at seam ends. Add sleeve mitts, opposite. Stitch shoulder seams. Add collar, opposite.

3) Place pressed edge of binding on seamline of overlap, *wrong* sides together; pin. For underlap, place pressed edge on seamline, *right* sides together; pin. Stitch overlap and underlap at neckline.

4) Fold the binding to inside of the garment, with fold on the seamline. Edgestitch binding over previous stitching; stitch to within 1" (2.5 cm) of neckline.

5) Pin overlap binding flat to inside of garment. Mark topstitching line on front side of overlap near the inside fold.

6) Topstitch through garment and binding, beginning at lower end of overlap (arrow); pivot at marked line, and stitch to neckline. Pivot; edgestitch around neckline through the garment and seam allowances, stretching slightly. Apply gripper snap at top of placket.

How to Attach a Mandarin Collar

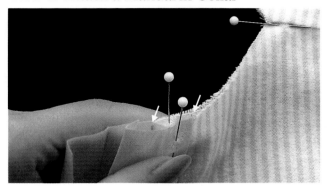

1) Cut ribbing for collar 2" (5 cm) wide and 2" (5 cm) shorter than neck opening. Fold in half lengthwise. Mark center back. Apply placket as in steps 1 and 2, opposite. Fold front, matching shoulder seams; pin halfway between placket seams (arrows) to mark adjusted center fronts.

2) Pin collar to neck edge at center back, with right sides together and raw edges even. Place pin on folded edge of collar ¼" (6 mm) from each short end. Match pins to center fronts; pin securely. Stitch collar to neck edge, stretching collar to fit. Trim collar to match neck edge. Complete placket, steps 3 to 6, opposite.

How to Add Sleeve Mitts

1) Cut ribbing for sleeve mitt 6" (15 cm) long on lengthwise grain and 1" (2.5 cm) wider than width of sleeve. Fold ribbing in half crosswise to 3" (7.5 cm), and lay under end of sleeve. Trim to match shape of sleeve. Stitch folded ribbing to wrong side of sleeve back at lower edge, using ¼" (6 mm) seam and matching raw edges. Turn mitt to right side.

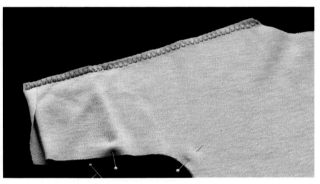

2) Pin kimono front to back at shoulder and underarm seams, right sides together. Fold hem allowance of sleeve front over finished sleeve back. Stitch shoulder and underarm seams.

3) Turn back hem allowance of sleeve front, encasing seam allowances. (Do not turn garment right side out.) Topstitch hem, stitching through sleeve back and mitt; use twin needle, if desired.

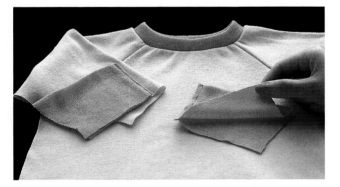

One-piece sleeve. Fold ribbing as in step 1, above. Cut mitt one-half the width of sleeve plus ¼" (6 mm). Stitch ¼" (6 mm) seam in one short end; turn seam to inside. Lay mitt on right side of back of sleeve, with seam at center; edgestitch short end at center. Stitch underarm seam. Turn hem allowance to wrong side. Topstitch hem as in step 3, left.

Buntings

A gusset applied at the lower edge of a kimono makes a bunting that covers the infant's feet and provides kicking room. For indoor use, make the bunting in the same fabric as that recommended for a kimono. For a warmer, outdoor bunting, use double-faced polyester fleece. To accommodate clothing worn under an outdoor bunting, use a kimono pattern one size larger than used for indoor buntings or kimonos.

Finish the neck of the bunting with a mandarin collar, or add a hood to the bunting if it is included in the pattern. For easy dressing, insert an 18" or 20" (46 or 51 cm) zipper. You may want to use zipper coil, which is available by the inch (2.5 cm) or in a 5½-yd. (5.05-m) package.

How to Make a Zipper Using Zipper Coil

1) Cut zipper 2" (5 cm) longer than garment opening. Mark bar tack placement 1½" (3.8 cm) from lower end of zipper. Open zipper about 1" (2.5 cm). Cut a notch to within ½" (1.3 cm) of mark for bar tack.

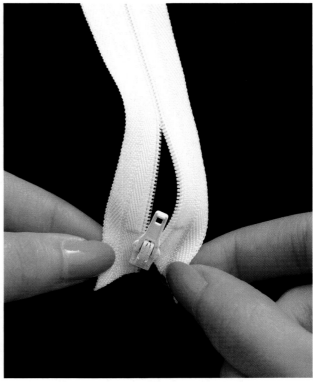

2) Insert one side of zipper coil into shaped end of zipper pull, with flat side of coil and tab of zipper pull facing up; insert other side, gently working coil into zipper pull.

3) Open coils above zipper pull. Partially close zipper. Bar tack by zigzagging in place over coil at placement mark to secure lower end of zipper.

4) Secure upper ends of coil with bar tacks ½" (1.3 cm) from ends. Zipper is ready to be applied to garment.

How to Insert a Zipper in a Bunting

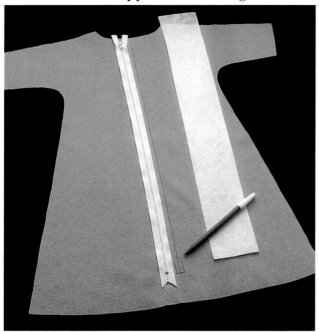

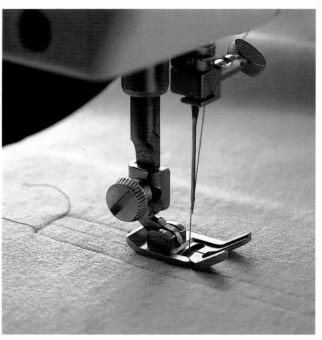

1) Mark line for zipper opening at center front from neck edge to zipper stop. Draw stitching box across lower end of line and ¼" (6 mm) on each side of line. Cut tear-away stabilizer 3" (7.5 cm) wide and 2" (5 cm) longer than zipper opening; glue-baste on wrong side of fabric under line for opening.

2) Staystitch across bottom line of stitching box; pivot at corner, and stitch to neck edge ¼" (6 mm) from marked line, using about 15 stitches per inch (2.5 cm). Repeat on other side of line, beginning at bottom line of stitching box.

3) Slash center line carefully to ¼" (6 mm) from bottom line; clip diagonally to, but not through, the lower corners.

4) Place one edge of zipper along edge of opening, right sides together, with zipper stop at bottom line of stitching box. With *garment side up,* stitch over previous stitching from zipper stop to neck edge, using zipper foot. Repeat for other edge, stitching from bottom to top.

5) Fold lower part of garment and stabilizer back at bottom of zipper, exposing the triangle of the stitching box and the end of the zipper tape. Double-stitch across triangle on the staystitching to secure triangle to zipper. Remove stabilizer.

How to Sew a Gusset in a Bunting

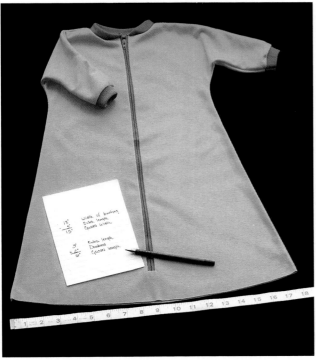

1) Complete bunting except for hem. The gusset adds 3" (7.5 cm) extra length to the bunting. For gusset width, subtract 3" (7.5 cm) from width of bunting at lower edge. The gusset length is 6" (15 cm), or double the extra length.

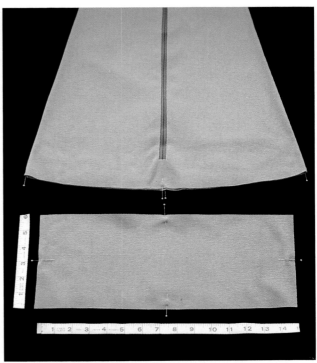

2) Cut a fabric rectangle for gusset according to the measurements, step 1, left. Divide edges of gusset and bunting into fourths; pin-mark.

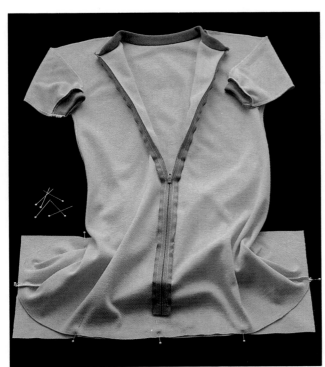

3) Pin bunting to gusset at marks, right sides together and raw edges even. Pin again halfway between pins, allowing bunting to curve naturally at corners.

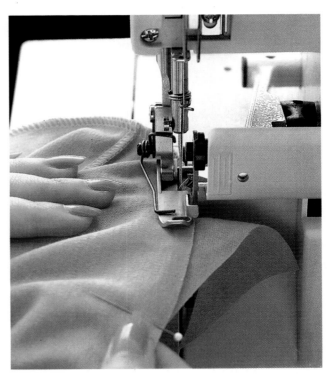

4) Serge or use three-step zigzag stitch for a ¼" (6 mm) seam around lower edge of bunting, using raw edge of bunting as a stitching guide. Serger knives will trim excess gusset fabric at corners; trim gusset before stitching if using three-step zigzag stitch.

Decorating the Nursery

When you plan the decor of a nursery, you may want to consider using neutral colors for wallpaper and paint. Save colorful decorating touches for the accessories, which can easily be changed or adapted as the child grows. Pastel colors are the traditional choice for a nursery, but do not overlook other choices, such as bold primary colors.

You can find many decorating ideas for nurseries in magazines, decorating books, and wallpaper and fabric stores. Select a theme to unify the nursery, and use your creative skills and sewing ability for projects such as appliqué, trapunto, or stenciling.

Patterns and kits are available for coverlets, bumper pads, diaper stackers, mobiles, wall hangings, infant seat pads, and toys. Sewing for the nursery can be even easier, using kits that include everything except the thread and filler. When using kits, there is no need for patterns, because the shapes are printed on the fabric. You may wish to embellish mobiles and wall hangings with buttons, ribbons, and pom-poms, and add fake fur to animal figures.

Nursery Accessories

Crib Kicker. Soft, stuffed, colorful shapes are joined with ribbon. Tie the crib kicker to the sides or end of the crib for the infant's enjoyment.

Mobile. Cut, sew, and stuff soft shapes. Tie them to a mobile hanger arm clamp. Attach the mobile to a crib or hang it from the ceiling over the changing table to entertain infants with color and motion.

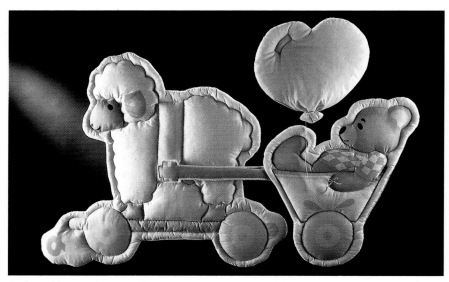

Soft Wall Hanging. Quilt a jumbo wall hanging by using a kit with preprinted fabric or by cutting a free-form shape around a printed design. Outline the design with machine quilting.

Diaper Stacker. Hang the diaper stacker in a convenient location. A heavy-duty hanger and cardboard bottom shape the fabric.

Crib Headboard and Side Bumper Pads. To make a crib safe and comfortable for infants, sew a padded headboard and bumper pads. Use 1" (2.5 cm) foam or polyester batting as padding. Make in separate pieces, and attach to crib with ties.

Fitted Crib Sheets

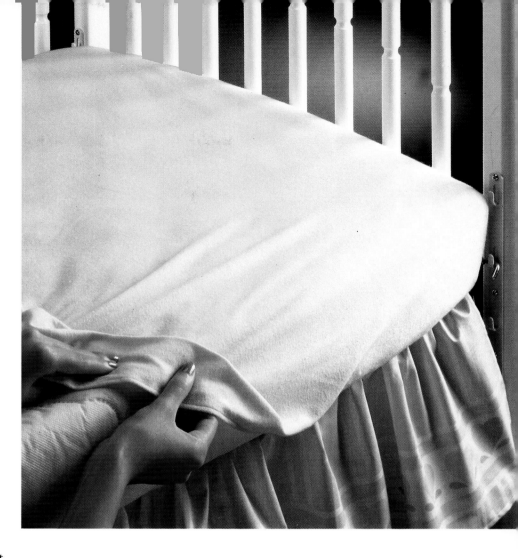

Fitted crib sheets can be coordinated with accessories such as bumper pads or coverlets. Interlock or jersey knit fabrics work best for comfort and stretchability.

Determine the fabric requirement for the size of your mattress. The fabric width equals the mattress width plus two times the depth plus 6" (15 cm) for seam allowances and fitted edge. The fabric length equals the mattress length plus two times the mattress depth plus 6" (15 cm). The square that is cut from each corner equals the mattress depth plus 3" (7.5 cm).

To fit a mattress of 27"×52"×5" (68.5×132×12.5 cm) for a six-year crib, cut a 43"×68" (109×173 cm) rectangle from 2 yd. (1.85 m) of 60" (152.5 cm) wide knit fabric. The width of the sheet should be on the crosswise grain or the grain with the greatest amount of stretch. Cut an 8" (20.5 cm) square from each corner.

How to Sew a Fitted Crib Sheet

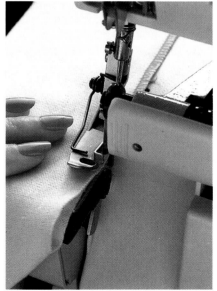

1) Cut square from each corner of sheet, as directed above. Fold sheet at each corner, with the right sides together and raw edges even. Stitch ¼" (6 mm) corner seam on a serger or use a narrow zigzag stitch on a conventional machine.

2) Cut two strips of ¼" (6 mm) wide elastic 3" (7.5 cm) less than width of mattress. On wrong side of sheet, pin center of elastic to center of each short end of sheet. Pin ends of elastic 6" (15 cm) beyond corner seams.

3) Serge or zigzag elastic to the raw edges, as in step 3, page 74. Continue stitching on edges between ends of elastic to finish all raw edges. Turn ¼" (6 mm) hem to wrong side of sheet, encasing elastic. Topstitch hem, stretching elastic.

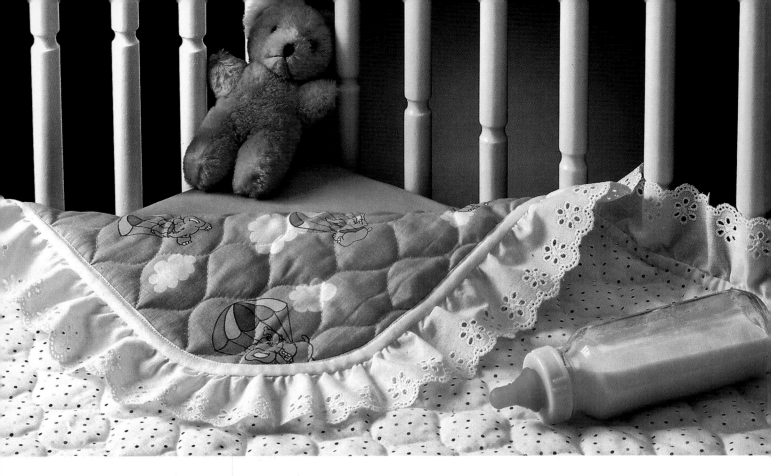

Crib Coverlets

Prequilted panels make the construction of a crib coverlet easy. These printed panels are about 45" (115 cm) wide and 36" (91.5 cm) long. Prequilted fabrics may also be used. Fabric layers usually include a cotton/polyester top fabric that is quilted to polyester batting. The backing may be brushed nylon tricot or a coordinating print or solid fabric of the same fiber content as the top fabric. To finish the panel edges, use either a pregathered trim and single-fold bias tape or a coordinating ruffle with attached bias tape.

Purchase the trim 5" (12.5 cm) longer than the distance around the panel. For easy application of the trim, round all corners of the coverlet, using a dinner plate to form the curve. Stitch around the coverlet a scant ¼" (6 mm) from the edges to secure the cut quilting threads and to make it easier to apply the trim.

How to Apply Pregathered Trim and Bias Tape

1) Pin trim on panel, with wrong side of trim facing underside of panel, beginning near one corner. Curve end of trim into seam allowance so ends overlap and finished edges taper to raw edge. Ease extra fullness into ruffle at corners, so ruffle lies flat when turned.

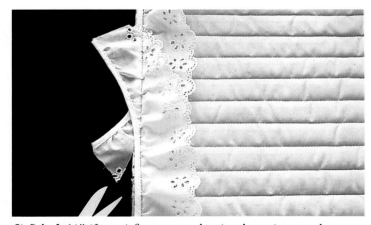

2) Stitch ¼" (6 mm) from raw edge (as shown) around panel to beginning of trim. Curve end of trim into seam allowance so ends overlap and finished edges taper to raw edge. Trim ends of pregathered trim even with panel edge.

How to Apply a Ruffle with Attached Bias Tape

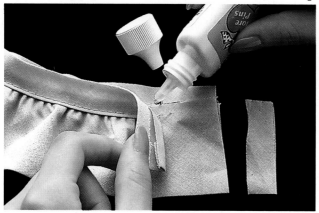

1) Remove stitching for 1½" (3.8 cm) on bias tape. Trim excess ruffle even with bias tape. Press ½" (1.3 cm) of ruffle and both tapes to inside. Glue-baste tapes to both sides of ruffle.

2) Insert edge of panel into bias tape, right sides up; pin. (Narrower bias tape or side with most attractive stitching is right side of trim.) Edgestitch tape to panel, beginning 1" (2.5 cm) from end of tape.

3) Stitch to within 2" (5 cm) from end. Cut excess trim, leaving ½" (1.3 cm); insert into the folded end of trim.

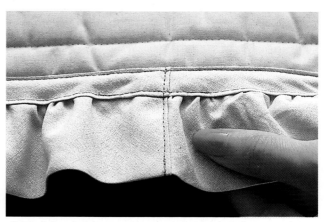

4) Finish stitching tape to panel, overlapping previous stitches. Stitch unstitched portion of other edge of tape, overlapping original stitching. Edgestitch ruffle and tape together at opening.

3) Open ½" (1.3 cm) single-fold bias tape; fold under ¼" (6 mm) at one end. Place tape foldline over trim, right sides together, on previous stitching; stitch in crease. Lap tape ½" (1.3 cm) over folded end to finish.

4) Turn tape to right side of panel, encasing raw edges of trim and panel. (It may be necessary to trim seam allowances.) Pin tape in place. Edgestitch free edge of tape to panel, matching needle thread color to tape, and bobbin thread to underside of panel.

Growing Up

Wardrobe Planning

Plan a child's wardrobe before you begin to sew. If the garments you sew are coordinated, they are more versatile and will have a different look with each ensemble. The child can easily select garments to wear together. Planning a wardrobe does not mean, however, that all garments must be made at one time.

Begin wardrobe planning by considering colors. Notice which colors are in style in ready-to-wear garments and which colors the child likes. Many garments and colors are suitable for either sex, so large portions of a wardrobe can be used by boys and girls.

Decide which colors will be central to the wardrobe. For basic wardrobe items, select colors and fabrics that can be worn year-round. Take swatches of fabrics with you when you shop. Garments for children do not take large amounts of fabric, so stockpile remnants in the wardrobe colors. You may want to purchase trims in coordinating colors for future use.

Wardrobe Basics

The core garments of a child's wardrobe include shirts, pants, overalls, a jacket, and for girls, a skirt and jumper. For sewing these core items, you may want to select a simple pattern that contains directions for sewing several garments, and vary the fabrics, trims, and finishes.

You can use one basic pants pattern for sweatpants, jeans with rolled cuffs, shorts, and pants with a mock fly. From a T-shirt pattern, you can make a shirt with a rugby placket and a pullover shirt with a kangaroo pocket. From one skirt pattern, make a skirt with a mock fly and another with a ribbing waistband. A simple yoked dress can be a school dress or a party dress, depending on the fabric.

Personalizing

To personalize simple pattern shapes, use coordinating fabrics for color blocking. Mix woven fabrics with knits. Sew the body of a shirt with a neck placket from a woven fabric, and the sleeves from a knit. Use piping to highlight the neckline, armholes, side seams, or pocket seams. Repeat trims, such as appliqués or buttons on shirts, to coordinate with pants or skirts.

Adding Durability

Build in durability as you construct children's garments. Seams and knees are subject to the most stress during dressing and active play, but both areas can be strengthened easily as you sew the garment.

Seams are most vulnerable at the crotch, shoulder, neck, and armhole. Strengthen the crotch and armhole seams with double-stitched, mock flat-fell, or edgestitched seams. Reinforce shoulder and neckline seams with decorative twin-needle seam finish (page 54), stitching before crossing with another seam. Machine-stitch hems for added strength in activewear (page 24).

The knee area wears out faster than any other part of a child's garment and is difficult to reach for repairs. Flat construction techniques allow you to reinforce knee areas as you construct the garment.

Patches

Tightly woven fabrics make the most durable patches. Interface, pad, or quilt patches for extra durability and protection at the knee, especially for crawling toddlers. Fuse the patch to the garment to make the application easier and to strengthen the patch.

Double-knee and decorative patches are cut according to the child's size. For infants, cut the patch 3½" × 4" (9 × 10 cm); for toddlers, 3¾" × 5" (9.5 × 12.5 cm); for children, 4½" × 6" (11.5 × 15 cm).

Round the corners of decorative patches to simplify application and to eliminate sharp corners that could catch and tear.

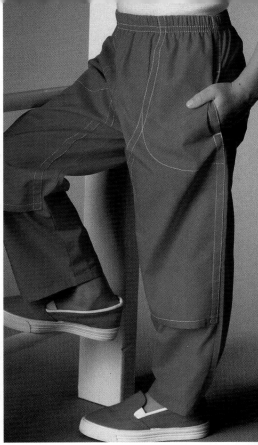

Double Knees. Apply double-knee patches (page 54) to the right side or the wrong side of the garment. The double layer of fabric adds strength to the knee area. You may also pad the area with polyester fleece, and machine-quilt, for extra durability.

Extended Pockets. An extended pocket (page 77) serves as both pocket and double knee, and is applied to right side of garment.

Decorative Knee Patches. For a decorative knee patch, use pinking shears to cut shapes from soft, nonraveling double-faced polyester bunting. Glue-baste in position, and topstitch to garment. Coordinate the color of the patch with ribbing or other trim. For a piped patch (page 55), select two coordinating fabrics for patch and piping. Quilt the patch fabric, if desired, before applying piping. Patches can be repeated on the elbows.

How to Reinforce Seams Using a Twin Needle

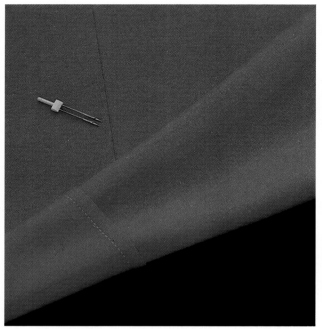

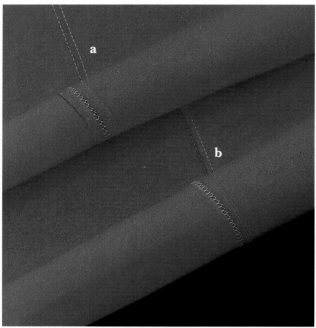

1) Stitch a plain seam. Press seam allowances to one side or open; trim to ¼" (6 mm). Insert twin needle in conventional sewing machine.

2) Stitch, centering seamline **(a)** between the two rows of stitching. For seam allowances pressed to one side **(b)**, you may prefer to stitch in the ditch with one needle as other needle stitches through garment and seam allowances.

How to Add Double-knee Patches

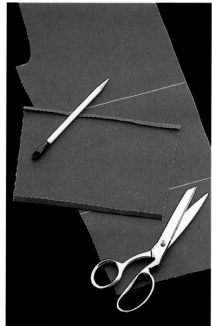

1) Cut two patches 6½" (16.3 cm) long and width of pattern at knee; press under ¼" (6 mm) on long edges. Mark placement lines on front of pants leg 3" (7.5 cm) above and below center of knee.

2) Cut polyester fleece to finished patch size; place on wrong side of patch, under ¼" (6 mm) seam allowances. Glue-baste patch in position over placement lines. Edgestitch long edges.

3) Machine-quilt patch to garment by topstitching through all layers, to provide extra strength. Construct garment according to pattern directions.

How to Add Decorative Knee Patches

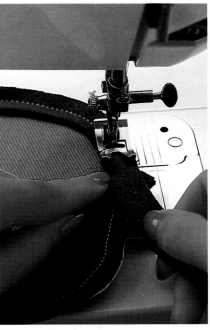

1) Cut two patches to size (page 52); round corners. Iron paper-backed fusible web to back of patches. Cut two strips of fabric for piping 1" × 24" (2.5 × 61 cm); cut on bias for woven fabrics or crosswise grain for knits.

2) Press strips in half lengthwise, wrong sides together. Stitch to right side of each patch, raw edges even, with ¼" (6 mm) seam allowance.

3) Curve ends of piping into seam allowance, so folded ends overlap and taper to raw edge. Trim piping even with raw edge of patch.

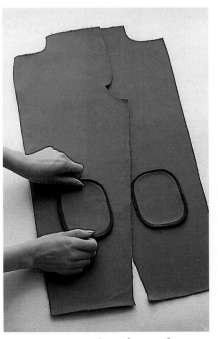

4) Trim seam allowance to ⅛" (3 mm). Press seam allowance to wrong side of patch, pulling piping out from patch. Remove paper backing from fusible web.

5) Fuse one patch to front of pants leg, parallel to hemline with center of patch slightly below center of knee. On the other pants leg, align second patch with first; fuse.

6) Stitch patch to garment, stitching in the ditch. Finish pants according to pattern directions.

Adding Grow Room

Build in grow room when you construct children's clothing, to get the maximum amount of wear from the garments. Without this extra room, a child going through a rapid growth spurt may be unable to wear a garment that is well liked and in good condition. The easiest place to add grow room is at the lower edge or sleeve hem. Rolled-up lined cuffs can be gradually lowered as the child grows. To add a coordinated look, select a lining fabric to match a shirt or other part of the ensemble. Cut lining on the straight grain or bias; add interest with a plaid or stripe. When sewing a garment that has straps, add extra length to the straps, and use overall buckles for easy length adjustment.

Ribbing. Make ribbing twice the recommended finished width. Fold the ribbing up, and gradually unroll it to add length as the child grows. Add ribbing to outgrown sleeves or pants legs by opening the hem and using the hemline for the new stitching line.

Inserts and trims. Planning carefully for balanced finished proportions, cut off the lower edge of the garment. Cut an insert of coordinating fabric, lace, or eyelet 1" (2.5 cm) wider than desired length, to allow for ¼" (6 mm) seam allowances on insert and garment. Stitch upper edge of insert to garment, then stitch lower section of garment to insert. Trims with finished edges can be stitched to the right or wrong side of a garment at the hemline for added length.

How to Add Lined Cuffs

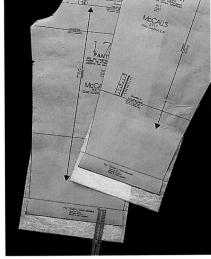

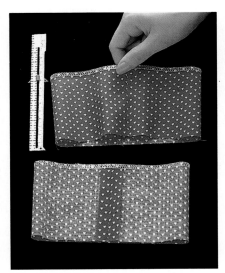

1) Adjust pattern at hem; lengthen hem allowance to 2½" (6.5 cm). Straighten side seams above original hemline for 4" (10 cm) to eliminate taper. Cut out garment; assemble according to pattern directions, but do not hem.

2) Cut two cuffs 3½" (9 cm) wide, and 1" (2.5 cm) longer than the circumference of finished sleeve or pants leg. Stitch short ends of cuff, right sides together, using ½" (1.3 cm) seam; press open. Serge upper edge, or turn under ¼" (6 mm), and press.

3) Stitch cuff to garment, with right sides together and raw edges even, using ¼" (6 mm) seam; match cuff seam to inseam. Turn cuff at stitching line, and press to wrong side of garment; topstitch at lower and upper edges. Fold cuff to right side.

Shirts

For a versatile shirt pattern, choose a loose-fitting, basic T-shirt style with a round neck. Using one pattern, you can make several shirts by varying the design with different neck, cuff, and hem finishes.

Fabric choices also add variety. Most loose-fitting T-shirt patterns may be sewn from lightweight knits and wovens for warm weather. Sweatshirt fleece or flannel make a warm shirt for cooler weather.

For easier sewing of a child's shirt, you may want to change the sewing sequence from the usual pattern directions. Do as much stitching as possible while the garment is flat. Pockets and appliqués are easier to apply before any seams are stitched. The flat method of ribbing application (page 35) is easier on Toddlers'

sizes, which have small neck and arm openings. The tubular ribbing application (page 60) is neater and may be preferred for Children's sizes.

Prefinished collars, cuffs, and waistbands are sold separately or in sets. They have a prefinished outer edge for a ready-to-wear look and are available in solid colors or in a variety of stripes and edge finishes. Prefinished collars, cuffs, and waistbands should be 1" to 3" (2.5 to 7.5 cm) smaller than the opening. If an appropriate child's size is unavailable, trim an adult size to fit. Use a prefinished collar for a T-shirt or for a shirt with a convertible collar. Use prefinished cuffs to finish a ribbed-top pocket.

How to Apply Prefinished Collar, Cuffs, and Waistband

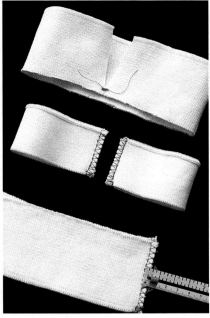

1) Trim short ends so collar, cuffs, and waistband are 1" to 3" (2.5 to 7.5 cm) shorter than garment edge; on collars, trim an equal amount from each end. Trim the width, if desired. Apply liquid fray preventer to short ends of collar.

2) Butt collar ends, and join with bar tack by zigzagging in place just inside neck seamline. Join short ends of cuff and waistband, using ¼" (6 mm) seam.

3) Divide collar, waistband, and garment edges into fourths; divide cuffs and sleeves in half. Place collar ends at center front, cuff seams at sleeve seams, and waistband seam at side seam. Attach as for ribbing, steps 2 and 3, page 60.

How to Apply a Prefinished Collar and Ribbing

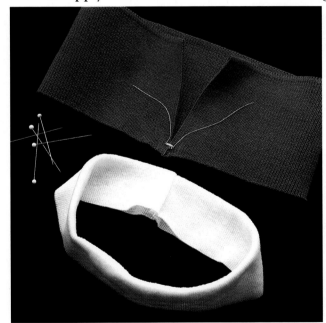

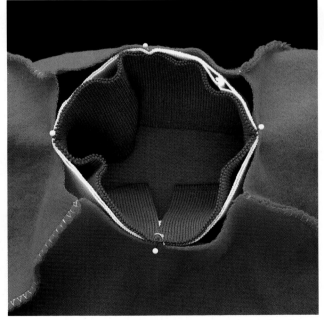

1) Trim prefinished collar, if necessary, as in step 1, above. Butt ends, and join with bar tack by zigzagging in place just inside neck seamline. Cut ribbing for narrow crew neck (page 17). Join ends, using ¼" (6 mm) seam; fold in half lengthwise, wrong sides together. Divide collar, ribbing, and neck edge into fourths; pin-mark.

2) Pin ribbing to right side of garment at neck edge, with pin-marks matching and raw edges even; position ribbing seam at back seam of raglan sleeve, at shoulder seam, or at center back. Pin collar over ribbing, with raw edges even. Place collar ends at center front. Stitch, stretching ribbing and collar to fit neck edge as in step 3, page 60.

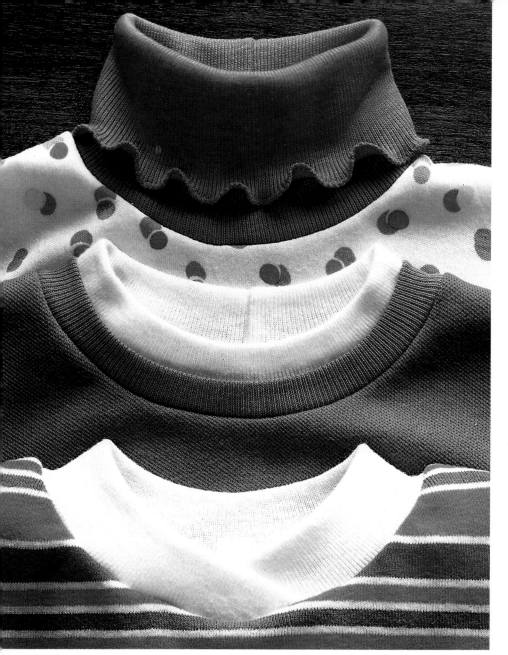

Ribbed Edges

Ribbing makes an attractive finish for necklines, cuffs, or waistlines on either knit or woven fabric. When using ribbing to finish a shirt made from woven fabric, check the size of the neck opening on the pattern to be sure the garment will fit over the child's head. Neck openings should be 1" to 2" (2.5 to 5 cm) larger than the child's head. It may be necessary to enlarge the opening or use a larger size pattern.

Ribbing does not have a right or a wrong side, so it can be folded with either side up. It can be applied using the flat method (page 35) or the tubular method, below. You can use the tubular method with large openings to produce a neater finish, because the seam that joins the ribbing into a circle is enclosed. Place the ribbing seam where it will be least visible.

For a double ribbing neck finish, combine two ribbings of different widths. For a lapped ribbing, cut a standard crew neck width, and lap the ends instead of joining them into a circle.

Lettuce edging can be used to finish the edge of the ribbing or knit fabric for a feminine look. Match the color of the thread to the fabric, or use a coordinating color thread.

How to Apply Ribbing Using the Tubular Method

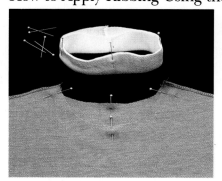

1) **Cut** ribbing two-thirds the length of neck opening; cut the width for standard crew neck (page 17). Join ribbing ends with ¼" (6 mm) seam. Fold the ribbing in half lengthwise. Divide ribbing and garment edges into fourths; pin-mark.

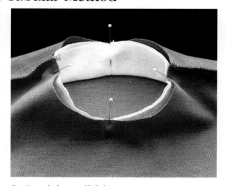

2) **Position** ribbing seam at center back or shoulder seam; pin ribbing to right side of garment, with raw edges even, matching pins.

3) **Serge** or use an overedge stitch (page 24) to apply ribbing to the garment, using ¼" (6 mm) seam; ribbing is on top and raw edges are even. Stretch ribbing between pins to fit garment.

How to Apply Double Ribbing

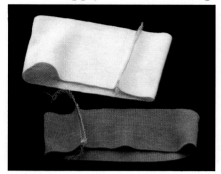

1) Cut two pieces of ribbing two-thirds the length of neck opening; cut one ribbing width for standard crew neck, and the other ribbing width for a narrow crew neck (page 17). Join short ends of each ribbing with ¼" (6 mm) seam.

2) Fold each piece of ribbing in half lengthwise, with wrong sides together. Pin narrow ribbing over wide ribbing, with raw edges even and seams matching. Divide ribbing and garment edges into fourths, and pin-mark.

3) Position ribbing seams at center back or shoulder seam. Pin ribbings to right side of garment, matching pins, with wide ribbing on top and raw edges even. Stitch as for tubular method, step 3, opposite.

How to Apply Lapped Ribbing

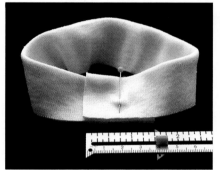

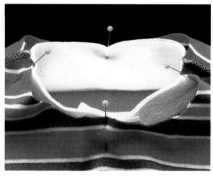

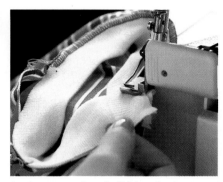

1) Cut ribbing two-thirds the length of neck opening plus 1½" (3.8 cm); cut width for standard crew neck (page 17). Fold in half lengthwise. Lap ends ¾" (2 cm); mark center of overlap with pin.

2) Divide ribbing and garment into fourths; pin-mark. Pin ribbing to right side of garment, with center of overlap at center front and raw edges even, matching pins.

3) Curve ends of ribbing into seam allowance, so folded ends overlap and taper to raw edges. Stitch as for tubular method, step 3, opposite, starting at center back.

How to Finish Ribbing and Knits with Lettuce Edging

Conventional method. Zigzag closely spaced stitches over ribbing fold or folded edge of hem, placing fold at center of presser foot and stretching the fabric as you stitch. The more you stretch the fabric, the more ruffled the edge will be. For hems, trim the hem allowance close to stitching.

Serged method. Adjust serger for rolled hem setting according to manufacturer's directions. Stitch along ribbing fold or folded edge of hem, stretching fabric as you stitch. Do not cut the folded edge with the serger knives. The more you stretch the fabric, the more ruffled the edge will be. For hems, trim hem allowance close to stitching.

Shirt Plackets

Add a placket on a close-fitting neckline for easier dressing. Placket openings can be used on knit and woven garments. To add variety to a shirt or blouse, combine woven and knit fabrics for the garment and placket. You can also coordinate the garments in a wardrobe by using coordinating placket fabrics.

Add hook and eye tape to a front slash. For a neat look when the placket is open, finish neck edges with twill tape or bias binding. Bind the neck in a matching or coordinating color.

Snap tape can add a decorative touch. For heavy fabrics and knits, use snap tape instead of buttons and buttonholes. It is easy to apply, and children can master snaps quickly.

Stitch fastening tapes carefully to maintain alignment of fabric design. If snap, hook and eye, or twill tape is not available in the color you need, dye the tape to coordinate with the garment fabric. Preshrink all tapes before applying them to garments.

How to Apply Hook and Eye Tape to a Shirt Placket

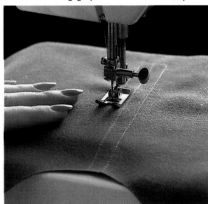

1) Mark a 6" (15 cm) center front line. Beginning at the neck edge, staystitch ⅜" (1 cm) from line. Pivot at lower end of placket, and stitch ¾" (2 cm) across; pivot again. Shorten stitches at the corners and across lower end. Continue stitching to neck edge.

2) Slash line to ¼" (6 mm) from lower end; clip to corners, step 3, page 40. Press under the seam allowances at staystitching. Cut hook and eye tape ½" (1.3 cm) longer than opening. Center tape in opening, placing first hook 1" (2.5 cm) below raw edge. Glue-baste, and edgestitch using zipper foot.

3) Join shoulder seams. Trim prefinished collar as in step 1, page 59. Stitch wrong side of collar to right side of garment at neck edge, with ends of collar at edges of tape. Bind neck seam with twill tape, as in steps 5 and 6, opposite.

How to Apply Snap Tape to a Full-length Shirt Opening

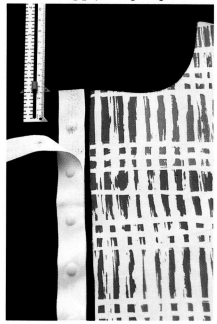

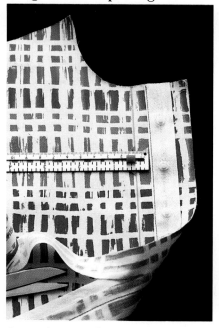

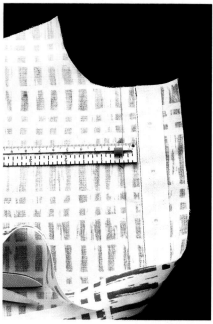

1) Cut the snap tape the length of the opening, with top and bottom snaps about 1" (2.5 cm) from raw edges. Press narrow double-fold hem to wrong side.

2) Mark center front on *right* side of *overlap*. Glue-baste tape to facing, with ball side up and tape edge 3/8" (1 cm) from center front. Edgestitch edge nearest center front, using zipper foot; at lower edge, turn under tape to match pressed hem. Trim facing to 1/4" (6 mm).

3) Mark center front on *wrong* side of underlap. Glue-baste tape to facing, with socket side up and edge 3/8" (1 cm) from center front. Edgestitch edge nearest center front, using zipper foot; at lower edge, turn under tape to match pressed hem. Trim facing to 1/4" (6 mm).

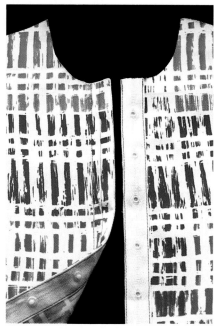

4) Turn ball side of tape to wrong side at stitched edge; turn socket side of tape to right side at stitched edge. Press lightly. Edgestitch free edges of snap tape to garment. Join shoulder seams. Trim prefinished collar as in step 1, page 59.

5) Attach collar as in step 3, opposite. Cut 3/4" (2 cm) twill tape 1" (2.5 cm) longer than neck edge. With right sides together and edges even, stitch tape to neck edge over previous stitching. At ends, fold tape to wrong side.

6) Fold twill tape onto garment, encasing the seam allowances. Edgestitch twill tape to garment; backstitch at both ends.

Rugby Plackets

A rugby placket can be added to a basic T-shirt to duplicate a ready-to-wear look. For a girl's garment, mark the placket opening to the left of the center to lap right over left. For a boy's garment, mark the placket opening to the right of center to lap left over right. The center front is at the center of the closed placket. The photos that follow show a girl's shirt.

Face the placket with self-fabric or a coordinating fabric. Interface the placket piece with fusible interfacing. Roll the overlap facing slightly to the outside for a decorative edge.

How to Sew a Rugby Placket

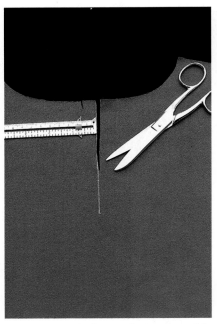

1) Cut placket facing 4½" (11.5 cm) wide by length of opening plus 2" (5 cm); interface. Finish long edges by serging or by stitching with 3-step zigzag. Mark 5" to 6" (12.5 to 15 cm) slash line on right side of facing, 1½" (3.8 cm) from one long edge.

2) Mark center front of garment with clip. Mark 5" to 6" (12.5 to 15 cm) slash line, ⅝" (1.5 cm) to left of center front for girls, right of center front for boys. Cut slash.

3) Pin facing to garment, right sides together, with facing edge ½" (1.3 cm) above neck edge and marked slash line on facing directly under garment opening. Narrow side of facing is on right front for girls, left front for boys.

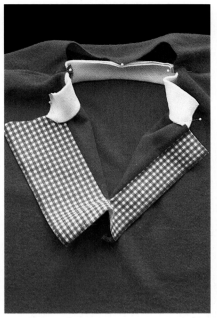

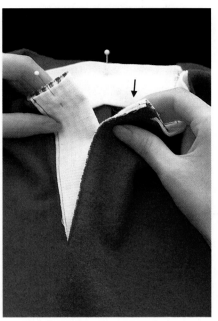

4) Stitch around slash on garment, ⅛" (3 mm) from raw edges, using 12 to 14 stitches per inch (2.5 cm). Shorten stitches near point; make two stitches across point. Cut facing at slash line; clip to stitching at point. Trim facing to match neckline curve.

5) Join shoulder seams. Turn facing to wrong side of garment. Pin collar to neckline, right sides together, so center backs match. Collar ends are ⅝" (1.5 cm) past seam of underlap and at center front mark of overlap.

6) Fold underlap in half, with right sides together. Fold overlap, right sides together, with placket seam about ⅛" (3 mm) from fold (arrow). Stitch neck seam; trim corners.

7) Cut ¾" (2 cm) twill tape for neck edge, so tape is long enough to overlap finished edge of each facing by ½" (1.3 cm). Pin tape over collar with right sides together and edges even; stitch over previous stitching. Turn facings to wrong side; turn tape over neck seam allowances, and pin to garment.

8) Stitch in the ditch (arrow) of underlap seam. Pin the overlap to the garment so about ⅛" (3 mm) of facing is visible at the fold; press. Stitch in the ditch of overlap seam, stitching from lower end to neckline; pivot, and topstitch ¼" (6 mm) from neck seam to secure tape.

9) Close placket; press. Stitch a rectangle ¼" (6 mm) long and the width of placket to secure all layers at lower end of placket. Make bar tack at point of slash by zigzagging in place. Trim excess facing below rectangle of stitching. Apply snaps, or buttons and buttonholes, at center front.

Pockets

Children like pockets, which can be both functional and decorative. Consider the pocket placement and size. Place pockets where the child can easily reach them, and make them large enough to hold objects.

Most styles and shapes of pockets can be used on shirts, jackets, pants, and skirts. Test the shape and size by using a template cut to finished size. Be creative with pocket placement, shape, and trim. Pockets are easier to attach before garment seams are stitched.

Add a kangaroo pocket to shirts and sweatshirts. A kangaroo pocket is a large patch pocket that has side openings. Sew this pocket into the side seams and waistline, and trim the upper edge with piping.

Ribbed-top pockets can be coordinated with knit collars and cuffs. To maintain the original pocket size, shorten the pocket by an amount equal to the finished width of the ribbing.

How to Sew a Kangaroo Pocket

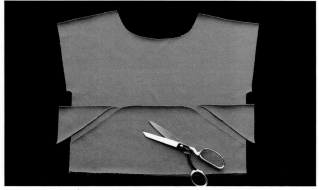

1) Cut pocket the same width as garment and half the garment length from neck edge at center front to lower edge. Cut hand openings at an angle from midpocket on the sides to one-third the width at the upper edge; round the corners at upper edge.

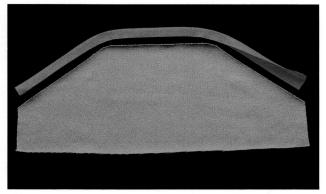

2) Cut fabric strip for piping, 1¼" (3.2 cm) wide and the length of upper edge of pocket; cut on crosswise grain for knits or on bias for wovens. Fold strip in half lengthwise, wrong sides together; press.

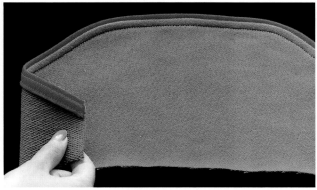

3) Stitch piping to right side of pocket at upper edge, raw edges even, using ⅜" (1 cm) seam. Press seam allowances to wrong side of pocket, with the piping turned up; topstitch the upper edge of pocket ¼" (6 mm) from seam.

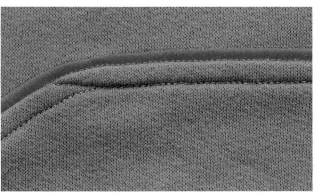

4) Glue-baste pocket on garment, matching side seams and lower edge. Topstitch upper edge of pocket, stitching over previous topstitching; do not stitch hand openings closed. Reinforce by stitching in ditch of piping seam; backstitch to strengthen ends.

How to Sew a Ribbed-top Pocket

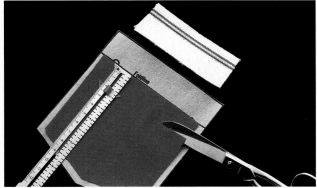

1) Cut pocket with ⅜" (1 cm) seam allowances at sides and lower edge. Trim pocket ¾" (2 cm) below finished upper edge. When using prefinished cuff, cut cuff ½" (1.3 cm) shorter than pocket width and 1¼" (3.2 cm) wide. When using ribbing, cut ribbing ½" (1.3 cm) shorter than pocket width and 2½" (6.5 cm) wide; fold in half lengthwise.

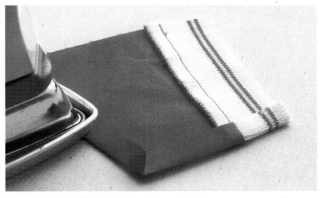

2) Stitch prefinished cuff or ribbing to upper edge of pocket, right sides together, using ¼" (6 mm) seam allowance; stretch cuff or ribbing to fit. Press seam toward pocket; press ⅜" (1 cm) to inside on lower and side edges of pocket. Finish as for basic patch pocket, step 3, page 79.

67

Exposed Zippers

You can add color to a shirt by inserting a nonseparating zipper so that the teeth are exposed. Zippers are available in a variety of colors and may be combined with a facing, rolled to the right side to resemble piping. Facings may be made in a contrasting color or a coordinating print, plaid, or striped fabric.

An exposed zipper is inserted in a slash opening in the front of a shirt. Neckline seams finished with twill tape or bias binding are durable, and the tape covers the neckline seam, which will show if the zipper is open.

How to Insert an Exposed Zipper

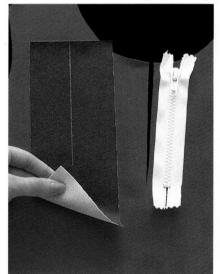

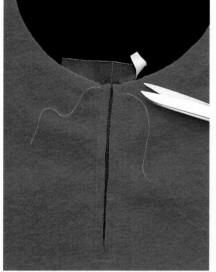

1) Mark center front of garment the length of zipper teeth, plus one seam allowance; slash. Cut facing 3½" (9 cm) wide and 2¼" (6 cm) longer than slash. Interface knit or lightweight facings; mark center line.

2) Pin facing to garment, right sides together, with ¾" (2 cm) above neck edge and marked line under slash. Stitch ¼" (6 mm) from slash, to ¼" (6 mm) below end of slash; pivot, and stitch ½" (1.3 cm). Pivot; stitch to neck edge. Trim excess facing at neck edge.

3) Cut facing on marked line; clip diagonally to corners. Serge or zigzag raw edges of facing. Turn facing to inside, rolling ⅛" (3 mm) of the facing to right side at slash line; press.

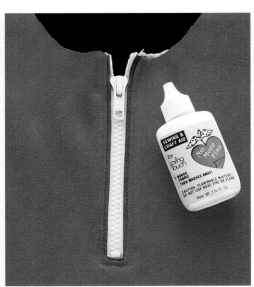

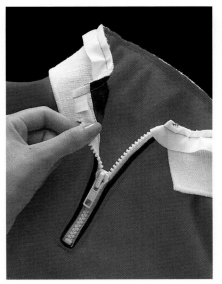

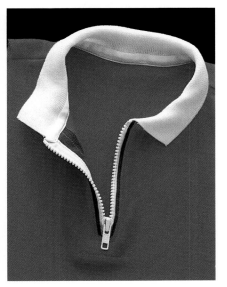

4) Center zipper under opening, with teeth exposed and zipper stop at lower end of opening; glue-baste. Topstitch, using zipper foot, ⅛" to ¼" (3 to 6 mm) from edge, through all layers. Stitch shoulder seams.

5) Apply collar with ends at edge of facing. Cut ¾" (2 cm) twill tape 1" (2.5 cm) longer than neck edge. Pin tape to neck edge, with right sides together and edges even; wrap ½" (1.3 cm) around zipper. Stitch over previous stitching at neck edge.

6) Fold the twill tape onto garment, enclosing the seam allowances. Edgestitch around outer edge of facing and lower edge of tape. Complete garment according to pattern directions.

Separating Zippers

Use exposed separating zippers as a decorative touch in children's sweatshirts or jackets made from warm, durable fabrics, such as corduroy, denim, sweatshirt fleece, and double-faced polyester bunting.

Before applying a zipper, complete the garment, including the collar and lower edge, according to pattern directions. Trim front opening seam allowances to ⅜"(1 cm), and trim the neck seam allowance to ¼" (6 mm). Finish neckline and zipper tapes with bias binding for a neat, decorative trim.

If the correct zipper size is not available, purchase a zipper longer than needed. The zipper can be trimmed to fit during application.

How to Apply a Separating Zipper

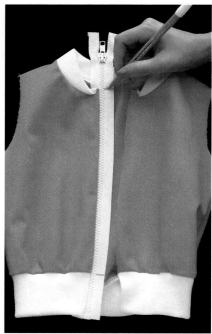

1) Trim neck and front opening seam allowances, above. Pin one side of open zipper to jacket edge, right sides together and edges even, with bottom stop at lower edge. Stitch next to zipper teeth from lower edge to neckline; leave excess zipper at neck edge.

2) Close zipper, and mark the alignment of seams or the fabric design. Open zipper. Matching marks on zipper to jacket, pin and stitch other side of zipper as in step 1.

3) Cut two bias strips (page 101), 2⅛" (5.3 cm) wide and 1" (2.5 cm) longer than zipper opening. Cut another bias strip, 1⅝" (4 cm) wide and length of neck edge. Press all strips in half lengthwise, wrong sides together.

4) Place binding over zipper tape, with raw edges of binding and zipper even. Wrap ½" (1.3 cm) of binding tightly around zipper at lower end; leave ½" (1.3 cm) excess binding at neck edge. Stitch from lower edge over previous stitching.

5) Pivot, and stitch along the neck seamline to fold of binding. If zipper is longer than opening, turn handwheel by hand to stitch between zipper teeth.

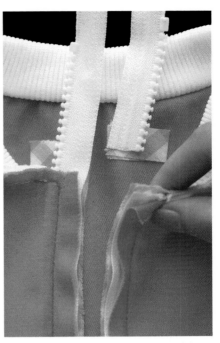

6) Trim excess binding even with raw edge of neckline. Trim excess zipper one tooth beyond stitching line. Repeat binding application for other side.

7) Place binding over collar, with raw edges even. Extend the ends of the neckline binding ¼" (6 mm) onto the zipper binding; trim excess. Stitch the neckline binding over previous stitching.

8) Fold bindings to the wrong side. Baste bindings to garment on fold. Edgestitch folded edge of binding to jacket front, beginning at the lower edge. Pivot at fold of the neckline binding.

9) Continue stitching around the fold of neckline binding and down other front binding fold. Bar tack at bottom of zipper by zigzagging in place.

Pants & Skirts

Pants and skirts are basic items in a child's wardrobe. The easiest pants and skirts to sew are those with elasticized waistbands.

For skirts and pants made of heavyweight fabrics, such as denim, corduroy, and sweatshirt fleece, use lightweight knit or woven fabric as a decorative, less bulky waistband. Good choices for a waistband are ribbing or knit fabric used with a sweatshirt fleece or corduroy garment, or bias-cut plaid flannel or shirting with a denim garment.

The directions that follow are for a pattern with a cut-on waistband. Cut the pattern apart below the waist foldline, ¼" (6 mm) less than the width of the elastic; the ¼" (6 mm) will be the garment seam allowance. Cut a waistband that is twice the width of the elastic plus ½" (1.3 cm) for two seam allowances. For woven fabrics, the length of the waistband should equal the waist measurement of the garment plus ½" (1.3 cm). For stretch knit fabrics or ribbings, cut the waistband 4" (10 cm) shorter than waist measurement of the garment.

Select elastic carefully; the amount of stretch and recovery varies with the type of elastic, the method of insertion, and the weight of the fabric (page 16). To determine the minimum length needed for a waistline, stretch the elastic around the widest part of the hips. Determine the maximum length by comfort. As a general rule, elastic will be 2" to 3" (5 to 7.5 cm) shorter than the waist measurement. Heavy fabric hinders elastic recovery; you may want to cut the elastic 1½" (3.8 cm) shorter than usual. Topstitch through the waistband and elastic to keep the elastic from twisting. Multiple rows of topstitching may be added, if desired.

How to Add a Coordinating Elasticized Waistband

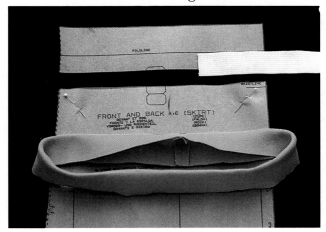

1) Cut pattern and waistband as directed, opposite. Join short ends of waistband with right sides together and using ¼" (6 mm) seam allowance; press open. Fold waistband in half lengthwise, wrong sides together. Complete garment except for applying waistband.

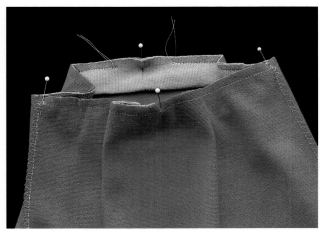

2) Divide waistband and garment into fourths; pin-mark. With seam at center back, pin both layers of waistband to right side of garment at pins; stitch ¼" (6 mm) seam, stretching knit waistband as you sew. Leave 2" (5 cm) opening at center back.

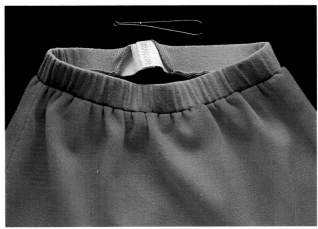

3) Cut elastic desired length plus 1" (2.5 cm). Insert into waistband, using a bodkin; lap ends ½" (1.3 cm). Stitch together securely.

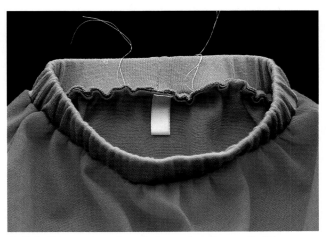

4) Stitch opening closed, inserting loop of ribbon to identify garment back; stitch over previous stitching. Finish seam allowances, if necessary.

5) Press seam allowances toward garment. Topstitch through garment and seam allowances from right side.

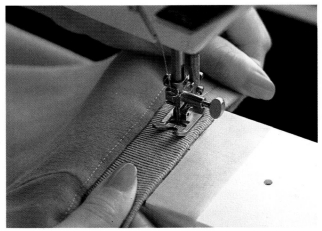

6) Topstitch waistband. Position presser foot at center of waistband. Mark guideline on machine with tape. Stitch waistband, stretching elastic as you sew.

Elastic Waistbands & Mock Fly

Apply elastic to the waistbands of pants or skirts. Use the stitched-on method for a comfortable finish that will not allow the elastic to roll or twist. For this method, use elastic with good stretch and recovery (page 16), so the waistband retains its fit. When stitching, stretch the elastic in front of the presser foot while holding the elastic taut behind the presser foot.

When using a pants or skirt pattern with a cut-on fly and elastic in the back waistband, you can save time by stitching a mock fly instead of inserting a zipper. You will need to eliminate the center front opening of the waistband pattern.

How to Apply Elastic to a Waistband

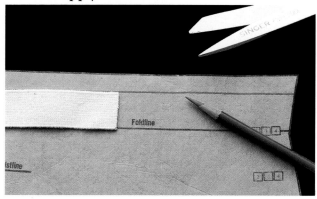

1) **Mark** new cutting line, above the foldline of the pattern, the width of the elastic. Cut and sew garment according to pattern directions, but do not apply elastic.

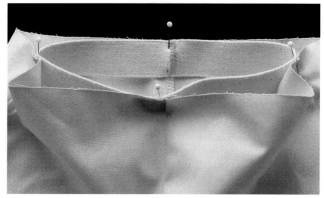

2) **Cut** elastic to fit snugly around hips; butt ends of elastic, and join with zigzag stitch. Divide elastic and garment edges into fourths; pin-mark. Pin elastic to wrong side of garment, with pins matching and edges even.

3) **Zigzag** or serge elastic to garment, stretching elastic between pins to fit garment; avoid cutting elastic when serging. Stretch elastic in front of presser foot, and hold taut from the back; do not pull fabric under the presser foot.

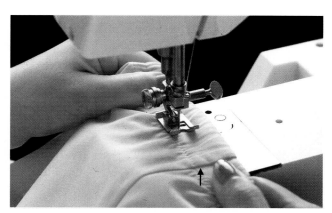

4) **Fold** elastic to inside, encasing elastic. Stitch in the ditch (arrow) from the right side at all seams. Topstitch at lower edge of elastic, stretching elastic to fit. Topstitch again ¼" (6 mm) inside first stitching; stretch elastic as you sew.

How to Sew a Mock Fly

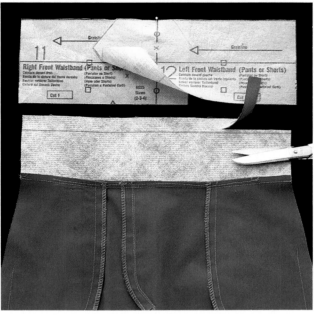

1) **Stitch** center front seam, right sides together; pivot at lower end of fly to stitch around outside of fly. Trim and finish seam; clip, and press. Press fly toward left front; topstitch fly through all layers at pattern marking.

2) **Lap** the front waistband patterns at center. Cut adjusted band; apply fusible interfacing. Stitch the waistband to garment front, right sides together; trim seam allowance, and press toward waistband. Trim seam allowance on other long edge to ⅛" (3 mm); finish by serging or using 3-step zigzag stitch.

How to Apply Elastic to a Back Waistband

1) **Adjust** pattern back at upper edge, as in step 1, opposite. Stitch and finish center back seam. Cut elastic 3" to 4" (7.5 to 10 cm) shorter than upper edge of pattern. With elastic on wrong side of garment and upper edges even, stitch ends to side seam allowances. Pin center of elastic to center back.

2) **Attach** elastic; fold to inside and topstitch as in steps 3 and 4, opposite. Pin side seams, right sides together. Turn front waistband over the back waistband at side seams; stitch seam.

3) **Turn** front waistband to inside, encasing ends of elastic. Clip back seam allowance below waistband; press seam open. Edgestitch around front waistband.

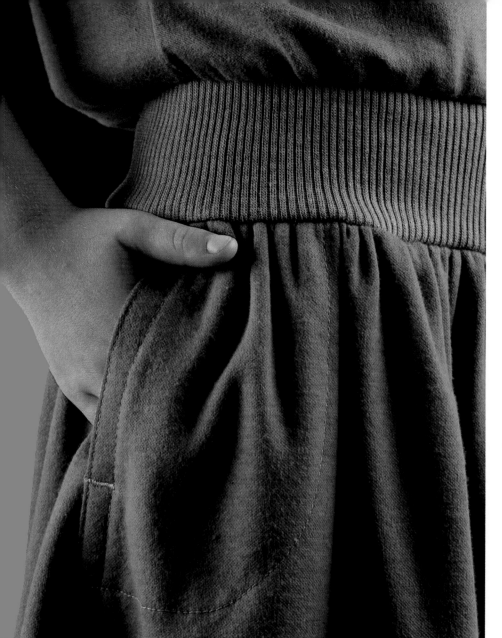

In-seam Pockets

Sew flat, nonbulky in-seam pockets in garment side seams for a ready-to-wear look. Adapt a pattern that has a two-piece pocket by cutting a single pocket piece from self-fabric. In-seam pockets may be either curved or rectangular.

An extended pocket (pictured on page 53) is applied to the outside of the pants and serves as a pocket and as a knee reinforcement. For a decorative touch, topstitch pocket in a coordinating color thread.

How to Sew One-piece In-seam Pockets

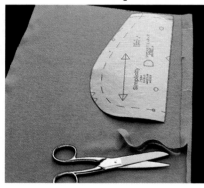

1) Mark pocket opening on side seam allowance of garment front; press to wrong side. Trim seam allowance to ¼" (6 mm).

2) Cut ½" (1.3 cm) twill tape 1" (2.5 cm) longer than pocket opening. Pin tape over trimmed seam allowance at pocket opening, with tape edge next to the fold; stitch through all layers on both edges of twill tape.

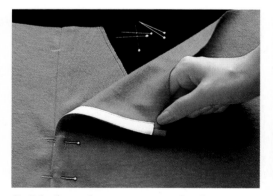

3) Stitch pocket to garment back at side seamline, with right sides together; finish pocket and seam edges. Press seam allowances toward pocket. Lap the garment front over the back side seam allowance, with taped edge even with seamline.

How to Sew Extended Pockets for Pants

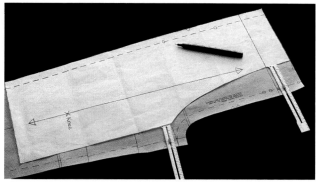

1) Place tissue on front pattern piece. Draw new pocket shape on tissue; begin at upper edge, 2" (5 cm) from center front, and curve to a point at crotch, 1¼" (3.2 cm) from inseam. Draw line from this point, parallel to grainline, to 4" (10 cm) below center of knee; draw line across to side seam. Transfer grainline and pocket opening marks.

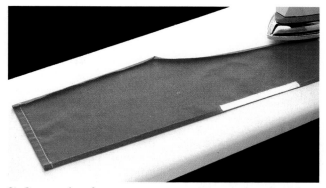

2) Cut pocket from new pattern. Topstitch a double ½" (1.3 cm) hem at the lower edge. Mark and finish edge of pocket opening as for one-piece in-seam pocket, steps 1 and 2, opposite. Press under a ¼" (6 mm) seam allowance on edges opposite pocket opening; clip curves.

3) Stitch pants front to pants back at side seam. Finish seam allowances; press toward the pants front. Glue-baste pocket over pants front, with the taped edge at seamline. Stitch pocket opening edge as in step 4, below. Topstitch edges opposite pocket opening.

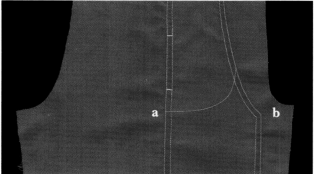

4) Mark a point on side seamline **(a)** opposite the crotch **(b)**. Curve line from this point to inner edge of pocket. Topstitch on this line to finish pocket. Repeat steps for other pocket.

4) Topstitch through all layers above and below pocket opening to match stitching lines on twill tape. Make a bar tack by zigzagging at each end of pocket opening.

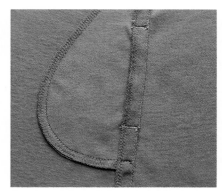

5) Pin and straight-stitch the loose edges of pocket to garment front. Repeat steps for other pocket.

6) Complete garment according to pattern directions. Catch upper edge of pocket in waistline seam.

Patch Pockets

Patch pockets can become a design element of the garment if they are made from a coordinating fabric. You may want to cut pockets from plaid fabric on the bias or from striped fabric on the crosswise grain when the garment is cut on the lengthwise grain. Pockets with straight edges are easier to sew. When adding trim to a pocket, apply it before stitching the pocket to the garment.

Create your own patch pockets of any size or shape, or use the pocket piece provided with the pattern. Check the size and placement of a pocket on the garment by cutting a pocket shape from paper; do not include seam or hem allowances. Mark the pocket placement on the garment with pins or washable marking pen. When creating your own pocket pattern, add seam allowances at the sides and lower edge, and a hem allowance at the upper edge.

A gathered or pleated patch pocket may be made by enlarging a patch pocket pattern. Because of the gathers or pleats, these pockets are more decorative and hold more than standard patch pockets.

How to Make a Basic Patch Pocket

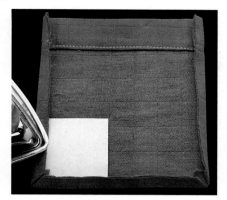

1) Determine finished pocket size; add ⅜" (1 cm) to sides and lower edge, and 1⅜" (3.5 cm) at upper edge. Cut pocket. Press upper raw edge under ⅜" (1 cm), then 1" (2.5 cm); stitch.

2) Place a 2" (5 cm) cardboard template at corner on seamlines. Press ⅜" (1 cm) seam allowances over template; open, and fold diagonally across corner to miter. Refold on pressed lines; press.

3) Glue-baste pocket in place on garment. Edgestitch sides and lower edge. Topstitch ¼" (6 mm) from previous stitching. To bar tack, zigzag at upper corners.

How to Make a Gathered or Pleated Patch Pocket

Gathered pocket. 1) Cut pocket 4" (10 cm) wider than basic patch pocket as in step 1, above. Finish upper edge with double-fold bias tape as in step 1, page 33.

2) Cut ¼" (6 mm) elastic 4" (10 cm) shorter than width of pocket; stitch to pocket 1⅜" (3.5 cm) below upper edge as in steps 1 and 2, page 82.

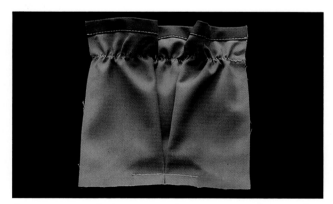

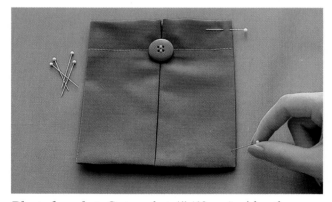

3) Press two 1" (2.5 cm) tucks to center at lower edge of pocket; staystitch. Press seam allowances, and attach pocket as for basic patch pocket, steps 2 and 3, above.

Pleated pocket. Cut pocket 4" (10 cm) wider than basic patch pocket, and finish upper edge as in step 1, above. Press two 1" (2.5 cm) pleats to center of pocket. Center and attach button 1" (2.5 cm) from upper edge, to secure pleats. Press seam allowances, and attach pocket as for basic patch pocket, steps 2 and 3, above.

Dresses

Choose construction methods that add a professional finish to the dresses that you sew. Line the yokes of dresses and blouses to eliminate facings that show through the fabric and to add stability to the yoke. Line lightweight or mediumweight fabrics with self-fabric, line bulky fabrics with a lightweight fabric, and line transparent print fabrics with solid-color fabrics. Use narrow French seams on sheer, lightweight fabric. They are used on straight seams, but are unsuitable for curved seams or seams with gathers.

How to Line a Yoke or Bodice

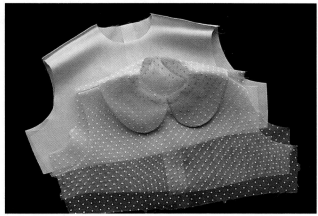

1) Cut yoke and yoke lining. Stitch shoulder seams, using French seams for sheer and lightweight fabrics. Attach collar to right side of yoke.

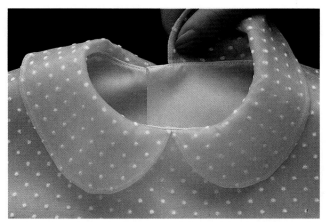

2) Stitch yoke to lining at neckline with right sides together, using short stitch length. Trim the seam allowances to a scant ¼" (6 mm); clip curves, and understitch seam allowances to lining. Turn; press.

3) Pin yoke to lining at lower edge; pin to skirt, right sides together, and stitch. Finish raw edges; press seam allowances toward yoke.

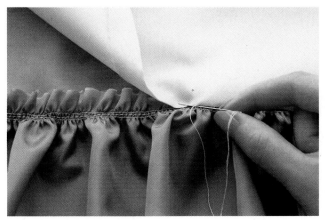

Alternative method. Stitch yoke to skirt, right sides together. Press seam allowances toward yoke. Turn under seam allowance of lining; slipstitch to seam.

How to Sew a Narrow French Seam

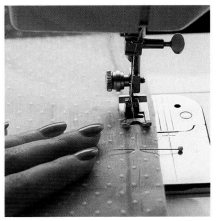

1) Mark stitching line in seam allowance, ³⁄₁₆" (4.5 mm) from the seamline. Stitch with *wrong* sides together, using 16 to 18 stitches per inch (2.5 cm).

2) Trim seam allowance to scant ⅛" (3 mm); press seam allowances to one side. Fold on stitching line, *right* sides together; press.

3) Stitch seam ⅛" (3 mm) from fold, encasing raw edges. Press seam allowance to one side.

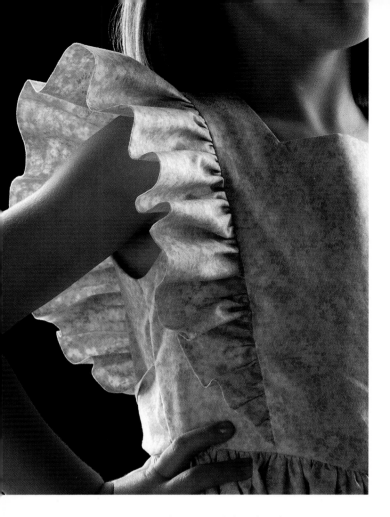

Gathers & Ruffles

Dress patterns often require the techniques of applying elastic, gathering fabric, and making ruffles. The methods that follow can simplify these techniques.

Transparent elastic may be substituted for elasticized casings to gather sleeves and waistlines. Stitch the elastic directly to the garment. The stitches are hidden in the folds of the fabric.

To create soft, fine gathers in lightweight fabrics, stitch gathering lines, using short stitches. To gather a long piece of fabric, you can zigzag stitch over a heavy thread or pearl cotton, which will not break when pulled.

Ruffles may be made from a double or single layer of fabric. Make double-layer ruffles from soft, lightweight fabrics. To cut, fold the fabric, and place the outer edge of the ruffle pattern on the fold to eliminate a hem. The doubled fabric adds body to the ruffle.

Make single-layer ruffles from firm fabrics or fabrics that show through when doubled, such as eyelets and sheer prints. When adding lace to a single-layer ruffle, you may want to reduce the pattern at the outer edge by the width of the lace.

How to Gather Sleeves with Elastic

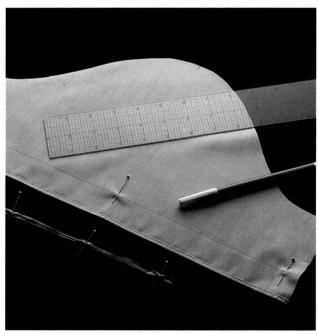

1) Cut ¼" (6 mm) elastic to fit the body comfortably plus seam allowances. Sleeve elastic does not need to fit snugly. Mark stitching line for elastic on wrong side of garment, using washable marking pen. For sleeves, pin-mark elastic and sleeve at seamlines and midpoint; for waistlines, divide elastic and garment into fourths, and pin-mark.

2) Pin elastic to wrong side of garment at pin-marks. Zigzag elastic to garment over marked line; stretch to fit between pins, but do not stretch elastic in seam allowances. Finish garment according to pattern directions, catching elastic in seam.

How to Gather Lightweight Fabrics

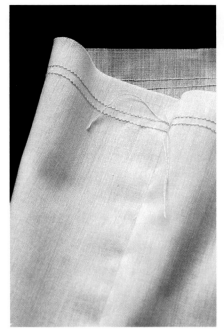

1) Loosen upper tension; set stitch length at 14 to 18 stitches per inch (2.5 cm). Stitch two gathering rows on right side of fabric, ⅛" (3 mm) apart, on each side of seamline.

2) Pull both bobbin threads, and distribute gathers evenly. Stitches automatically pull to wrong side of garment for gathering ease. Wrap threads around a pin to anchor at each end.

3) Stitch on seamline between rows of gathering when joining to garment. Do not remove gathering stitches; outer row of stitches is hidden in fabric fullness.

How to Make Ruffles

Double-layer ruffle. 1) Fold fabric, wrong sides together; place outer seamline or hemline of the ruffle pattern on fold. Cut ruffle. Using a wide zigzag setting, stitch ½" (1.3 cm) from raw edges over a heavy thread.

2) Pull heavy thread, and distribute gathers evenly. Wrap thread around a pin to anchor at each end. Stitch ruffle to right side of garment; remove heavy thread.

Single-layer ruffle. Stitch flat lace to outer edge of ruffle, wrong sides together. Trim seam allowance to ¼" (6 mm); press toward ruffle. Edgestitch ⅜" (1 cm) ribbon over seam allowances through all layers. Gather ruffle.

Closures

For children's activewear select closures that are decorative, functional, and easy to handle. To prevent tearing, interface closure areas that use buttons, snaps, hooks and eyes, and hook and loop tape.

Apply gripper snaps to shirt plackets, waistbands, and jacket openings. Mark snap placement carefully, and double-check the markings before applying the snaps; removal is difficult and may leave a hole in the garment. Two kinds of tools are available for attaching gripper snaps: the attaching tool and the fastener pliers. The attaching tool requires hammering and should be used only on a solid surface. Strike firmly, rather than tapping lightly. The pliers can be used for most sizes of snaps. Snaps and pliers must be made by the same manufacturer.

Use buttons with buttonholes or button loops to decorate garments. Button loops may be made from strips of knit or woven fabric. Cut knit fabric loops on the lengthwise grain; cut woven fabric loops on the bias grain.

Hook and loop tape is available in circles, squares, or strips, and is easy for children to use. For a shirt opening, use circles or squares. For a waistband, use a strip of tape at least an inch (2.5 cm) long. Self-basting hook and loop tape is backed with an adhesive. Position the tape, and press it on with a finger before stitching. Close hook and loop tape before laundering to prevent lint accumulation on the tape and snags in other garments.

Tips for Applying Closures

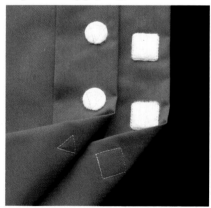

Hook and loop tape. For squares and strips, edgestitch, overlapping stitching at ends. For circles, stitch triangles. Cover stitching on right side with appliqué or button, if desired. Adhesive from self-basting tape can coat the needle; clean needle with alcohol.

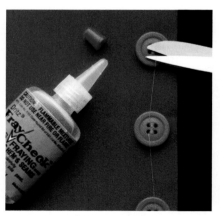

Buttons, sew-on snaps, and hooks. Attach button foot; cover or lower feed dogs. Adjust zigzag stitch width for distance between holes; stitch, ending with several stitches in one hole to anchor. Attach all closures with continuous thread; clip threads, and apply liquid fray preventer.

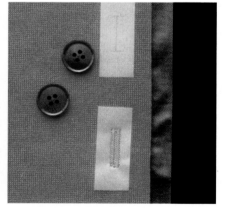

Buttonholes. Use water-soluble stabilizer under the buttonholes when sewing knit fabrics. Position transparent tape over buttonholes; mark buttonhole length on tape. To prevent puckers, set stitch length longer than for woven fabrics. Stitch over tape, parallel to ribs of knit.

How to Apply Button Loops

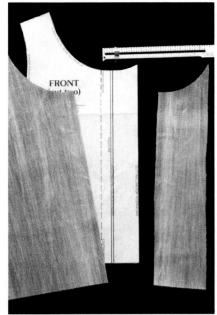

1) Trim pattern front lengthwise ⅝" (1.5 cm) from center front; cut garment fronts. Cut facings 2⅝" (6.8 cm) wide and the length of garment; trim facings to match shape of garment at neck edge.

2) Cut fabric strip 1" (2.5 cm) wide for loops; strip length equals length of loop, step 3, right, times number of loops needed. Add 2" to 3" (5 to 7.5 cm). Trim one end to a point; insert into bias tape maker. Press raw edges to meet at center.

3) Fold strip in half lengthwise; edgestitch, stretching strip as you sew. Cut strip into pieces, each twice the button diameter plus 1⅜" (3.5 cm). Fold pieces in half; baste loops to center front, matching raw edges. Stitch shoulder seams; attach collar.

4) Stitch facing to garment, with right sides together and with loops between facing and garment; use ⅝" (1.5 cm) seam. For bulky fabrics, trim seam allowances. Turn facing to wrong side of garment; press.

5) Understitch on right side of facing, close to seamline, through facing and both seam allowances. Stitch other facing to front of garment; understitch.

6) Topstitch garment ¼" (6 mm) from the front and neck edges. Complete garment. Butt center fronts of finished garment; mark button placement at center of loops. Attach buttons.

Personalizing

Adding a Personal Touch

Use your imagination to create personal touches that will make a garment special to the child. The techniques for personalizing clothing can be adapted to a single garment or repeated on several garments in a coordinated wardrobe.

Consider color blocking, especially when you are sewing more than one garment; use the remnants from one garment for blocks of color in another. Or highlight and coordinate garments with piping. You may want to add appliqués; purchase them ready-made, or design your own. Trapunto, an appliqué variation, can be used to add dimension to a garment.

Patchwork trims can add greatly to the cost of ready-to-wear garments, but some techniques permit you to make designs with small amounts of fabric in a short time. Fabric paints may be used to personalize a garment. They can also be used to decorate fabric shoes.

When personalizing children's garments, remember that special touches can be added to fronts, backs, and sides of garments, and all trims must be attached securely and safely.

Tips for Placement of Design

Balance design shapes. For example, you can offset a small design at the upper left of a shirt with a larger design at the lower right.

Place a placket at a shoulder or raglan seam so a design can be centered on a shirt front.

Add a design to the back of a shirt that has a plain front, or repeat a design used on the front.

Machine-stitch trim to sleeves while the piece is still flat to eliminate the need for handwork in areas too small for your sewing machine to reach.

Decorate sleeves using elbow patches or by placing designs down the center of the sleeve.

Highlight shoulder seams with piping, twill or bias tape, or ribbing.

Repeat a design to make a border at the neckline, yoke, or hemline.

Create interest with fabric strips or trims placed diagonally, vertically, or horizontally; an uneven number of strips or trims may be more pleasing than an even number.

Appliqués

Appliqués are a traditional method for decorating children's garments. Select from three basic types of appliqués; purchase iron-on or sew-on appliqués, or design your own. For a fast and easy decorative touch, fuse purchased iron-on appliqués to a garment, following the manufacturer's directions. Purchased sew-on appliqués may be fused to the garment using fusible web. You may wish to topstitch to secure the appliqué through many launderings.

You may want to design your own custom-made appliqués. Look at magazines, ready-to-wear garments, or coloring books for ideas. Fruit, animals, numbers, toys, hearts, and rainbows are all popular shapes for children's appliqués. Consider cutting motifs from printed fabrics.

Before assembling the appliqué, plan the work sequence. Smaller pieces may need to be positioned on and stitched to larger pieces before applying appliqué to the garment, and some pieces may overlap other pieces.

Embellish the appliqués with bows, buttons, ribbons, pom-poms, fabric paint, or cord. Cut ends of cord may be placed under appliqué pieces before fusing. Trims may be stitched or glued in place, using permanent fabric glue.

Tips for Appliqués

Practice stitching an appliqué on a test piece before working with the garment piece.

Select a colorfast fabric for an appliqué that is compatible with garment fabric in weight and care requirements; preshrink all fabrics.

Remember that it is easiest to stitch around large, simple shapes with few corners.

Leave a fabric margin in a geometric shape around intricate motifs cut from printed fabrics.

Apply paper-backed fusible web to the wrong side of the appliqué fabric before cutting out the shape.

Add durability to a garment by applying an appliqué with fusible web at knees or elbows.

Add ½" (1.3 cm) to sides of appliqué pieces that will go under another piece; trim to reduce bulk when final placement is determined.

Remember that shapes drawn on paper backing of fusible web will be reversed on the garment; draw mirror images of letters or numbers.

Apply tear-away stabilizer to the wrong side of a garment for smooth satin stitching at the edge of an appliqué.

Use a special-purpose presser foot with a wide channel to prevent buildup of satin stitches.

Apply an appliqué to garment before joining seams. It is easier to apply an appliqué while fabric is flat.

How to Make and Apply an Appliqué

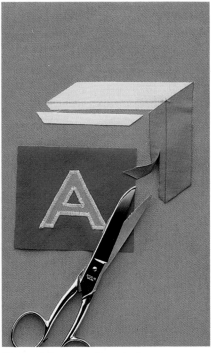

1) Apply paper-backed fusible web to wrong side of appliqué fabric, following manufacturer's directions. Allow fabric to cool.

2) Draw design on fabric or paper backing; add ½" (1.3 cm) to sides of appliqué pieces that go under another piece. Cut out design and remove paper backing.

3) Position appliqué pieces on the garment fabric. Trim appliqué pieces under other pieces to reduce bulk; leave scant ¼" (6 mm). Fuse appliqué pieces to garment.

4) Cut tear-away stabilizer 1" (2.5 cm) larger than appliqué. Glue-baste to the wrong side of garment, under appliqué. Zigzag stitch around appliqué, using short, narrow stitches.

5) Decrease the upper tension, and adjust stitches for short, wide zigzag; satin stitch around appliqué edges to cover all raw edges. Remove tear-away stabilizer.

Appliqué with squeaker. Apply fusible interfacing to wrong side of appliqué. Place squeaker under appliqué; glue appliqué in place at edges. Complete appliqué as in steps 4 and 5, left.

Appliqué Techniques

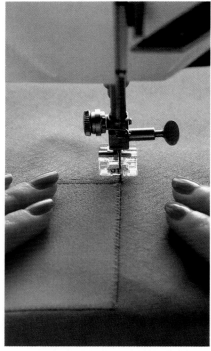

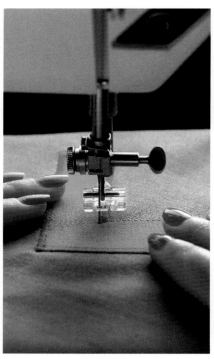

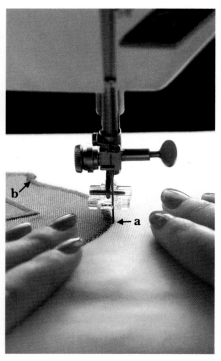

Outside corners. Stitch past the edge of the appliqué one stitch. Raise presser foot, pivot fabric, and continue stitching.

Inside corners. Stitch past corner a distance equal to width of satin stitch. Raise presser foot, pivot fabric, and continue stitching.

Curves. Pivot fabric frequently. For outside curves, pivot with needle on outer edge of stitching (**a**); for inside curves, pivot with needle at inner edge of stitching (**b**).

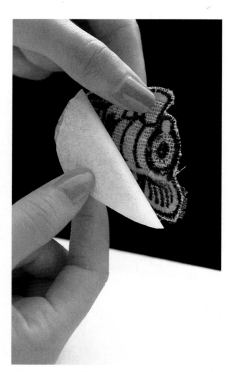

Appliqués from printed fabric. Cut designs from fabric to use as appliqués. For an intricate design, cut a fabric margin in a simple shape.

Decorated appliqués. Decorate an appliqué with buttons, bows, bells, ribbons, or pom-poms. Attach the decorations with permanent fabric glue, or stitch securely.

No-sew appliqués. Place purchased appliqué face down on paper; apply slightly larger piece of paper-backed fusible web to appliqué. Remove paper backing and excess web at edges. Fuse; topstitch if desired.

Trapunto Appliqués

Trapunto is a method for padding an appliqué to give it a three-dimensional look. Traditional trapunto techniques consist of applying the appliqué to the right side of the fabric, slashing the backing fabric, stuffing with fiberfill, and closing the slash, using hand stitches.

To achieve the same three-dimensional look, use the easy alternate method that follows. Experiment with the amount of fiberfill; small amounts work best. After stitching, fuse the appliqué to the fiberfill to stabilize the padding through laundering and wear.

How to Sew a Trapunto Appliqué

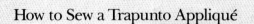

1) Prepare fabric as for appliqué, steps 1 and 2, page 91. Do not fuse appliqué to garment.

2) Glue-baste stabilizer to wrong side of garment. Zigzag appliqué to the garment with short, narrow stitches; use a screwdriver to lightly fill appliqué with fiberfill just before stitching is completed.

3) Satin stitch as for appliqué, step 5, page 91. Pierce appliqué with a pin; distribute fiberfill evenly. Remove stabilizer. Lightly press appliqué to fuse fiberfill to the web; do not press flat.

Fabric Painting

Fabric paints can be used to decorate garments. Wash and dry fabric to remove sizing before applying the paint. Help children to plan and practice their own designs before they begin painting on fabric. Or trace an existing picture onto fabric, and then paint it. Fabric paints may be combined with iron-on transfers or appliqués. Decorate the fabric before cutting out the pattern, or decorate the completed garment.

Select acrylic fabric paints for projects painted by children. The cleanup of these water-soluble paints is easy while the paint is wet. Most paints require four hours or longer to dry.

Create different looks with four types of fabric paint: stencil, slick, puff, and glitter. Stencil paint dries with a matte, washed look; set this paint permanently with heat. Use slick paint for a wet-looking, plastic surface; it does not require heat setting. Puff paint lacks luster and is flat when first applied; however, it rises and assumes a soft, marshmallow texture when heated with an iron. If garments will be washed by machine, apply puff paint in thin layers; thick layers of paint require hand washing. Glitter paint sparkles when dry and does not require heat to set.

For paints in tubes or accordion bottles, shake the paint into the applicator tip before using, to eliminate air bubbles. Apply it with steady, even pressure to prevent puddles.

Follow the manufacturer's directions for application of paint. Allow one color to dry before overlapping it with a second color or stencil. After the paint is completely dry, press to heat-set, if recommended by the manufacturer, using a press cloth. Lay garments flat when painting, and place wax paper between layers to prevent liquids from bleeding through the fabric layers. Launder painted garments inside out and use fabric softener to keep paints soft and flexible.

How to Stencil on Fabric

1) Place the garment flat on clean paper, with wax paper between fabric layers. Use purchased stencil design or cut an original design from thin cardboard. Tape stencil in position on garment.

2) Dilute stencil paint, using one drop of water to ten drops of paint. Dampen sponge; squeeze until almost dry. Dip sponge in paint, and use to paint inside stencil. Lift stencil gently. Heat-set according to manufacturer's directions.

Alternative method. Cut sponge into desired shape. Dampen the sponge; squeeze until almost dry. Dip sponge in paint, and apply to garment. Allow garment to dry flat. Heat-set according to the manufacturer's directions.

Techniques with Fabric Paint

Hold paint tubes 2" (5 cm) above the fabric to paint dots, squiggles, and zigzags. For dots, hold tube still, and squeeze. For squiggles and zigzags, move tube steadily, and squeeze continuously. Heat-set paint if recommended by manufacturer.

Dilute paint with water for colored splashes. A solution of one part water and ten parts paint produces a good consistency. Wet brush with paint, and gently shake over fabric to decorate large areas of fabric quickly. Heat-set paint if recommended by manufacturer.

Use puff paint or slick paint to outline shapes or write words. Outline fused appliqué to seal raw edges; paint replaces all stitching. For puff paint, heat with an iron, following manufacturer's directions, to cause puffing.

Use a child's hand for printing on fabric. In shallow pan, mix paint solution of one drop water and ten drops paint. Dip hand in paint; place on fabric. Press down on fingers and palm; lift hand straight up. Heat-set paint if recommended by manufacturer.

Color & Design Blocking

Create a distinctive look with color and design blocking. Choose two or more fabrics to use in one garment; plan the fabric arrangement, and cut individual pattern pieces from each fabric. Or trace a pattern piece, cut the traced pattern apart, and cut each piece from a different fabric. Choose a simple pattern design. For variety, you can mix woven and knit fabrics, or solids and prints. Combine colorfast fabrics that are compatible in weight and have similar care requirements.

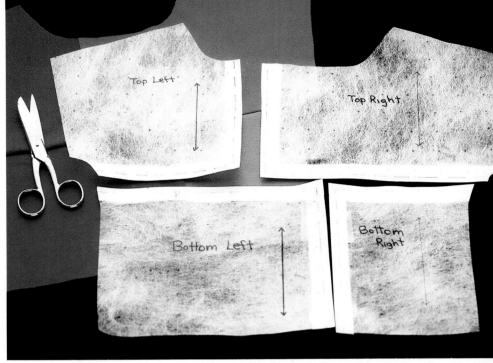

Adapt a pattern. Divide the pattern piece into sections by drawing new seamlines; cut pattern apart, and add ¼" (6 mm) seam allowance at new seams. Join sections before completing the garment.

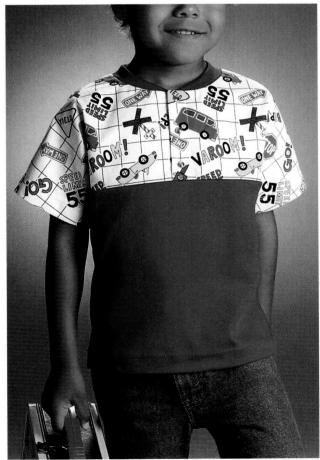

Combine woven and knit fabrics. When using a pattern designed for knit fabric, use woven fabric in areas that will not affect wearing ease, such as collars, cuffs, yokes, and pockets.

Combine striped fabrics. Cut pattern pieces from two or more striped fabrics, each with stripes of a different size. Combine stripes horizontally, vertically, or diagonally.

Patchwork Trims

Versatile patchwork trims can be made from small amounts of woven fabrics. Use coordinating colors and the garment fabric, if desired, for diagonal or Seminole patchwork trims. Stitch the fabric strips together on the straight grain for either type of trim. Diagonal patchwork trims can be constructed faster, and from less fabric, than Seminole patchwork trims.

Constructing Seminole patchwork trims is not difficult, but this method of piecing does require precise measuring, cutting, and stitching. A rotary cutter and ruler help you to cut strips accurately.

To vary the size of Seminole patchwork trims, vary the size of the squares. For a border, sew wide strips at the edges, or cut a border strip on the straight grain, and sew it to the Seminole patchwork trim.

Diagonal or Seminole patchwork trims may be applied to garments in several ways. Insert them as stripes or garment borders, or use color blocking techniques (page 97). An entire yoke, bib, or other pattern piece may be cut from a patchwork trim.

How to Make a Diagonal Patchwork Trim

1) Cut fabric strips on straight grain the finished width plus two ¼" (6 mm) seam allowances. Cut two strips each of three or more fabrics; widths of strips may vary. Stitch strips together lengthwise, with right sides together and in desired sequence, repeating the pattern once.

2) Press seams in one direction. Cut pieced fabric into bias strips, and stitch strips together as necessary, step 2, page 101. Attach to garment, being careful not to stretch strip.

How to Make a Seminole Patchwork Trim

1) Measure, and cut fabric strips on straight grain the finished width plus two ¼" (6 mm) seam allowances. Join strips in sequence, right sides together; stitch accurate seams. Press seams in one direction.

2) Cut pieced fabric into strips. The width of each strip should be equal to the width of center strip as cut in step 1, left.

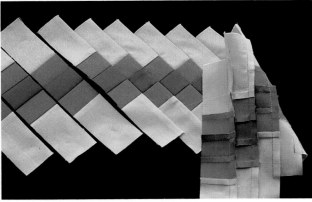

3) Join strips, right sides together; use ¼" (6 mm) seams and stagger color blocks to form diagonal pattern. Alternate direction of seam allowances on strips to help match seams. Edges along sides are staggered. Press seams in one direction.

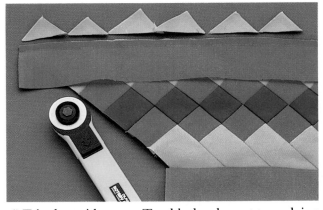

4) Trim long sides even. To add a border, cut two edging bands of straight-grain self-fabric or coordinating fabric; stitch to long sides of patchwork trim, right sides together.

Piping

Piping adds a decorative touch at garment seams or edges. Use it on pockets, collars, side seams of pants and skirts, shirt yoke seams, and seams of raglan sleeves. Combine piping with color blocking (page 97) and topstitching for interesting effects.

Make piping from either woven or knit fabric. Cut woven fabric on the bias; cut knit fabric on the crosswise or lengthwise grain. Use fabric that is colorfast and requires care similar to that of the garment. Preshrink fabric and the cord or yarn used as the filler in the piping.

Before cutting the fabric strips for piping, decide whether the piping will be filled or flat. For a soft, yarn-filled piping or a firmer, cord-filled piping, the fabric width should be at least two seam allowances plus the circumference of the filler, plus ⅛" (3 mm). For a flat ⅛" (3 mm) piping, cut the width of the fabric strip at least two seam allowances plus ¼" (6 mm). The finished piping seam allowances should be the same width as those of the garment. When using ¼" (6 mm) seam allowances on the garment, it is easier to sew the piping with ⅝" (1.5 cm) seam allowances, and trim them later to match the garment.

How to Sew Piping

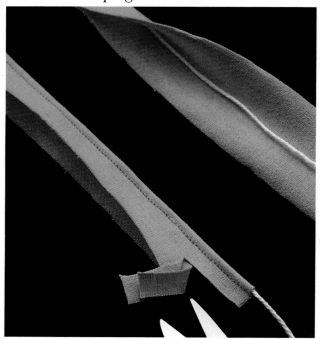

Filled piping. 1) Center cord or yarn on wrong side of fabric strip. Fold strip in half lengthwise, wrong sides together, enclosing cord. Stitch close to cord, using zipper foot; stretch woven fabric slightly as you sew. Trim seam allowances to match those of garment.

2) Pin piping to right side of garment, with raw edges even. Curve ends of piping into seam allowance at inconspicuous place, so ends overlap and piping tapers to raw edge. For enclosed seams, such as collar seams, taper piping into seam allowance at intersection of seams, step 2, page 118.

How to Prepare Bias Strips

1) Fold fabric diagonally, so straight edge on crosswise grain is parallel to selvage. Cut on fold for first bias edge. Use ruler and rotary cutter to cut 2" (5 cm) strips.

2) Piece strips, if necessary. Pin strips in V shape, with right sides together and short ends aligned. Stitch ¼" (6 mm) seam; press seam open. Trim seam allowances even with bias strip.

Single-fold bias tape. Prepare bias strip, left. Trim one end to a point. Pull bias strip through bias tape maker; press folds to center as strip comes out end of tape maker.

3) Stitch on seamline. Remove stitching in piping at ends; trim cord in seam allowance. Stitch garment seam over previous stitching line, with piping between right sides of garment pieces.

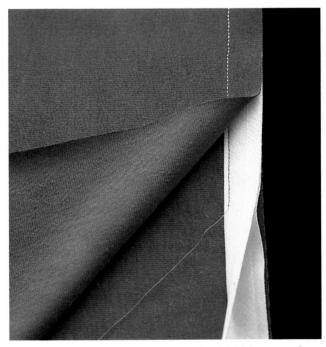

Flat piping. Use 1" (2.5 cm) single-fold bias tape for ⅛" (3 mm) finished piping and ⅝" (1.5 cm) seam allowances. Press tape open; fold in half lengthwise, and press. Pin piping to garment, and stitch seam as in steps 2 and 3, left.

Dressing Up

Machine Heirloom Sewing

Heirloom sewing adapts French hand sewing to machine methods. Although an heirloom project still takes patience, practice, and careful work, with modern sewing machine technology you can now master techniques that were formerly done by hand. Projects can include small items, such as a bonnet; parts of a garment, such as a blouse yoke; or a total garment.

Basic heirloom techniques consist of joining strips of fabrics and trims. Strips may be placed either horizontally or vertically on the garment piece. The fabric strips are cut or torn on the straight grain to the length needed; it is easiest to use the crosswise grain. The width of the strips may vary as long as the proportions are pleasing. Fabric strips may be machine-embroidered, using a wing needle and machine embroidery thread; gathered on both sides to form a puffing strip; or pin-tucked, using a twin-needle and pin-tuck presser foot.

Use fine woven cotton or cotton blends in sheer fabrics, such as batiste and broadcloth. Select from three weights of 100 percent cotton Swiss batiste. All will wrinkle, which is part of the effect of these fabrics. Lightweight Swiss batiste is sheer enough to allow the color of a slip to show through. The batistes that are easiest to work with are the mediumweight and heavyweight fabrics. Imperial® batiste is an economical polyester/cotton blend that is wrinkle-resistant and is available in several colors.

Laces and trims of 100 percent cotton, or of 90 percent cotton and 10 percent nylon, feel soft and are easiest to handle. You may use insertion laces, which have two straight edges; edgings, which have one scalloped edge; or beadings, which have woven holes to accommodate ribbon trims. Use double-faced satin ribbon in beading and for ties. In heirloom sewing, entredeux is always used between fabrics and laces to reinforce seams decoratively. Entredeux resembles hemstitching with seam allowances on both sides.

How to Design an Heirloom Project

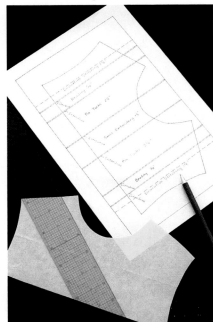

1) Make a full-size pattern piece from tissue. Trace onto firm paper. Plan design, using fabrics, trims, and entredeux; widest trim should be at the center, fabric strips at the curved edges, and the entredeux between fabric and trims.

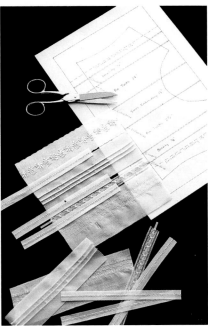

2) Measure pattern at its widest and longest points. Cut all strips 1" (2.5 cm) longer than width or length, depending on the direction of the strips. Sew pin-tucks, decorative stitching, or puffing strips, if used (pages 108 and 109).

3) Join fabrics, laces, and trims (pages 110 and 111) to form a rectangle or square. Block fabric to original shape by pinning in place and steaming to set. Let cool. Cut garment piece.

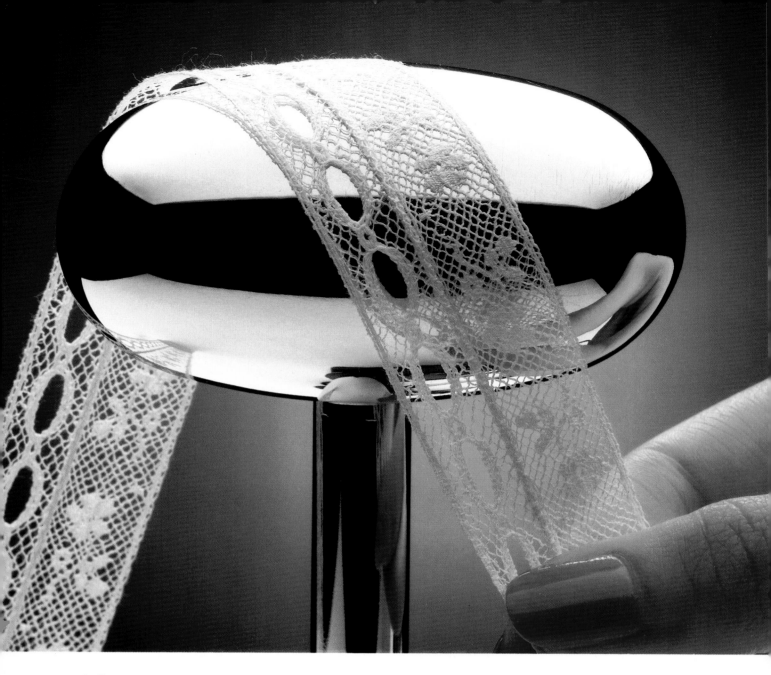

Heirloom Techniques

You may want to practice heirloom techniques before making your project. To produce different looks and designs, creatively combine the methods that follow. For pressing convenience, set up a puff iron near your sewing machine. Use spray starch on both sides of the fabric and trim, except for puffing strips, and press over the puff iron to make fabric easier to handle. Some pieces, such as the puffing strips, cannot be ironed once they are sewn.

When sewing fine, soft fabric, laces, and trims, use an extra-fine thread that will not add bulk to the seams. Use cotton machine embroidery thread on the conventional sewing machine; use extra-fine cone thread on the serger. White thread is appropriate for white, ecru, and pastels. The fine thread blends into the fabric.

A size 8 (60) or 9 (65) needle is recommended because it is compatible with the fabric and thread. Stitch length is determined by the distance between the holes of the entredeux. Stitch width will vary depending on the technique.

A new needle is an essential for machine heirloom sewing. Check frequently for burrs on the needle point. Change the needle after every five hours of use, even if the needle point feels smooth.

How to Prepare Straight-grain Fabric Strips

Swiss cotton. Clip into selvage. Pull a thread across to other selvage; cut fabric on pulled thread line. Clip selvage and pull another thread across fabric at desired width or length of fabric strip; allow for two ¼" (6 mm) seams in the width.

Polyester/cotton batiste. Clip selvage and tear fabric. Clip again and tear at desired width or length of fabric strip; allow for two ¼" (6 mm) seams in the width. Press edges of strip flat. Edges may be trimmed, using ruler and rotary cutter; serger knives will trim fibers.

How to Set Machine Stitch Length

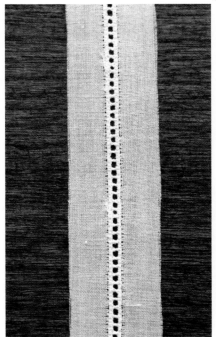

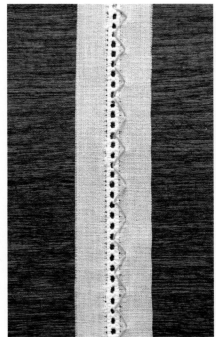

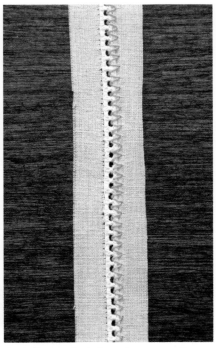

1) Cut entredeux strip about 4" (10 cm) long to use for determining stitch length. Set machine for a zigzag stitch 3 mm wide and for a length of 12 to 16 stitches per inch (2.5 cm).

2) Stitch so the swing of the needle zigs into the middle of a hole of the entredeux and zags into the batiste seam allowance.

3) Adjust stitch length so needle zigs into each hole of the entredeux. Once the stitch length is established, it will remain the same for the entire project.

Heirloom Strips

Fabric strips for machine heirloom sewing may be embellished with machine embroidery and pin tucks, or gathered for puffing strips.

Machine embroidery is the easiest technique to use. Experiment with wing needles, decorative stitches, and machine embroidery thread.

Make pin tucks, using a pin-tuck presser foot and a twin needle. Twin needles are sized according to the distance between needles and the thickness of the needles. Use a 1.8 (70) or 2 (80) needle for fine fabrics. The fabric strip should be wider than the finished width to allow for the fabric that forms the tucks. Make an uneven number of tucks, with the middle tuck at the center.

Create puffing strips by gathering both sides of a fabric strip before joining it to entredeux. Cut fabric to the desired width plus ½" (1.3 cm) for two seam allowances, and one and a half times the finished length. Set the zigzag stitch length (page 107); set the stitch width to zigzag over ⅛" (3 mm) of the edge of the fabric. Press, but do not starch, the fabric strip before gathering; do not press after gathering.

How to Machine-embroider Using a Wing Needle

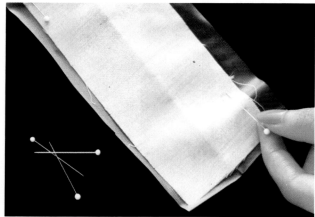

1) Cut fabric to desired width plus ½" (1.3 cm) for two seam allowances. Apply spray starch to fabric strip; press. Fold strip lengthwise; lightly finger press fold to mark stitching line. Pin a strip of water-soluble stabilizer to back of fabric.

2) Stitch one or more rows, using a decorative stitch and a wing needle. Remove stabilizer according to manufacturer's directions; press fabric strip.

How to Roll, Whip, and Gather a Puffing Strip

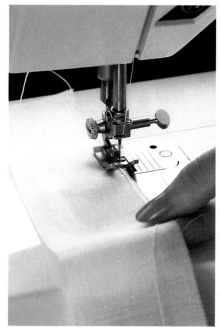 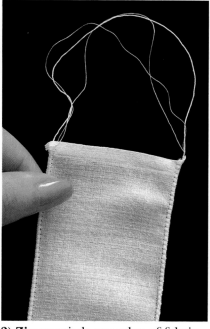 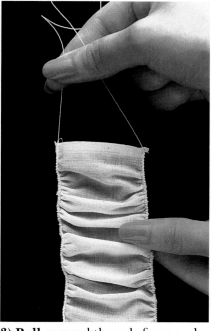

1) Cut fabric and set stitch length and width, opposite. Place a thread along edge on right side of fabric, leaving a 3" (7.5 cm) thread tail. Zigzag stitch over thread; fabric will roll over thread.

2) Zigzag stitch one edge of fabric. Turn fabric, and leave a 4" (10 cm) loop of thread before stitching down other side. Leave 3" (7.5 cm) thread tail at end.

3) Pull encased threads from each end to evenly gather both sides of puffing strip. Gather to desired length; distribute gathers. Knot gathering threads at each end.

How to Sew Pin Tucks

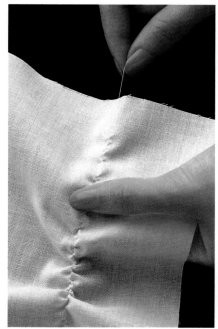  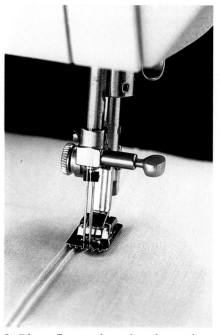

1) Cut fabric strip about 2" (5 cm) wider than finished width. Pull thread lengthwise on strip to mark position for center tuck. Tighten upper thread tension slightly; set stitch length to 12 to 14 stitches per inch (2.5 cm).

2) Apply spray starch to fabric strip; press. Using pin-tuck presser foot and twin needle, stitch over pulled-thread mark; hold the fabric taut. Bobbin thread draws two needle threads together, creating pin tuck.

3) Place first tuck under channel of pin-tuck presser foot; determine distance from first tuck by channel selection. Stitch additional tucks. Trim equal amounts on each side of strip, allowing for ¼" (6 mm) seam allowance on each side.

Joining Heirloom Strips

Join fabric strips, laces, and trims for heirloom sewing with a narrow seam that is neat and durable. Machine methods closely duplicate traditional hand stitches but are much faster to do and easier to master. For additional strength, use entredeux between fabrics and laces or trims. Use spray starch on all strips except puffing strips. Press all strips before stitching.

Several techniques are used for joining strips. One of the joining techniques used in heirloom sewing is rolling and whipping. This technique rolls a tiny amount of fabric around the adjoining lace or trim, adding strength to the seam. When applying flat lace to a hem edge, press the seam allowance toward the fabric. You may also want to edgestitch through all layers. A rolled seam sewn on the serger produces the same result as rolling and whipping.

The narrow zigzag stitch on a conventional sewing machine or the flatlock stitch on a serger may be used to join two laces with finished edges. Use a narrow zigzag stitch to join trimmed entredeux to lace with finished edges.

Gather laces before joining them to trimmed entredeux. Pull a heavy thread in the lace heading to create gathers or, if the lace lacks a heavy thread, machine-stitch a gathering line. Trim the remaining seam allowance on the entredeux and use entredeux with gathered lace to highlight a yoke seam or neck edge (page 113).

Selecting Joining Techniques

Edges to Be Joined	Conventional Machine	Serger
Entredeux to puffing strip	Rolled and whipped seam	—
Fabric to entredeux	Rolled and whipped seam	Rolled seam
Fabric to flat lace	Rolled and whipped seam	Rolled seam
Lace to entredeux	Zigzag seam	—
Lace to lace	Zigzag seam	Flatlock seam

How to Gather Lace and Join to Entredeux

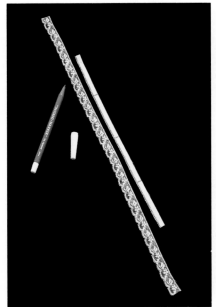

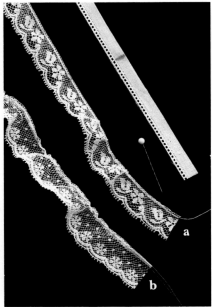

1) Cut entredeux 1" (2.5 cm) longer than needed; trim away one seam allowance. Cut flat lace 1½ times longer than entredeux. Divide lace and entredeux into fourths; mark.

2) Pull heavy thread in lace heading from both ends to gather lace (**a**). For laces without a heavy thread, stitch next to lace edge, using 14 to 16 stitches per inch (2.5 cm); pull bobbin thread to gather (**b**). Match marks on lace and entredeux.

3) Set zigzag stitch length (page 107). Butt trimmed entredeux edge to lace; zigzag 1" (2.5 cm) at a time, using a narrow stitch. Use a small screwdriver to hold gathers under presser foot. Continue to end; remove gathering thread.

How to Use the Rolled and Whipped and the Rolled Seam Joining Methods

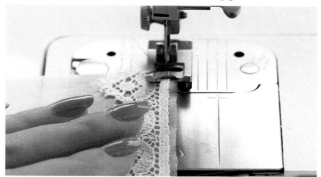

Roll and whip fabric to flat lace. 1) Set zigzag stitch length (page 107). Lay starched and pressed strips, right sides together, with bottom strip extending ⅛" to ³⁄₁₆" (3 to 4.5 mm) beyond top strip.

2) Set zigzag stitch width so left swing of stitch is ⅛" (3 mm) from edge of top strip and right swing of stitch extends over edge of bottom strip. As needle moves to the left, edge of bottom strip rolls over seam; upper thread tension may need to be loosened.

Roll and whip fabric to entredeux. Set zigzag stitch length (page 107). To join entredeux and flat fabric **(a)**, place starched and pressed strips right sides together and raw edges even; stitch in the ditch next to the entredeux holes. Trim seam allowances to scant ⅛" (3 mm). To join entredeux to a puffing strip **(b)**, trim entredeux seam allowance to scant ⅛" (3 mm); position strips, and stitch in the ditch. Remove the gathering thread. Finish both seams as in step 2, above.

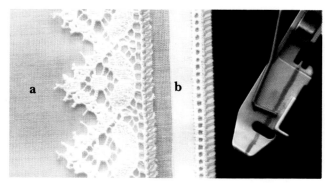

Rolled seam. Adjust serger for rolled hem setting, following manufacturer's directions; set stitch length at 2 to 3 mm. Stitch lace to fabric **(a)**, with right sides of strips together and raw edges even. To stitch entredeux to fabric **(b)**, mark line from needle position to end of presser foot (arrow). Use line as a guide to stitch in the ditch next to holes of entredeux.

How to Use the Zigzag and Flatlock Joining Methods

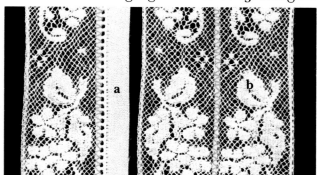

Zigzag seam. Set zigzag stitch length (page 107); set width for narrow stitch. For entredeux **(a)**, trim one seam allowance and butt trimmed edge to lace; stitch. For laces **(b)**, place right side up and butt edges; stitch.

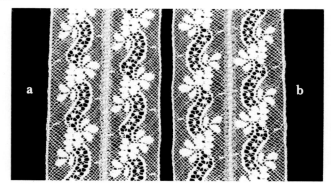

Flatlock seam. Adjust serger for flatlock stitch following manufacturer's directions. Stitch; pull laces flat. Ladder of stitches **(a)** shows on right side when laces are stitched with right sides together. Trellis of stitches **(b)** shows on right side when laces are stitched with wrong sides together.

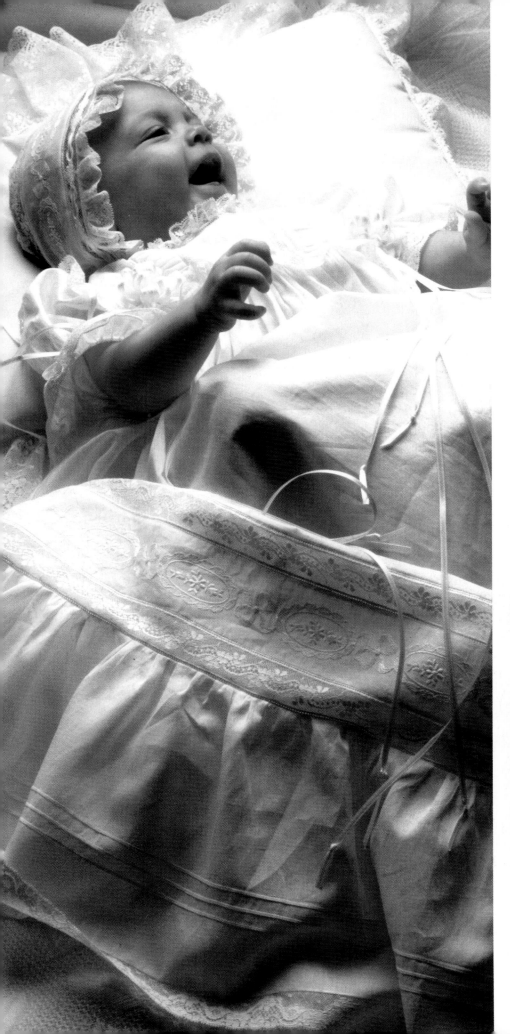

Sewing an Heirloom Dress

Any dress or blouse pattern with a yoke may be adapted to machine heirloom sewing. Read about machine heirloom techniques (pages 105 to 111) before sewing an heirloom garment.

Plan an heirloom design to fit the yoke. When using Swiss cotton, line the yoke to support the fabric. Interfacing, which shows through sheer fabric, may be eliminated.

A variation of the yoke design may be used for a bonnet or as an heirloom band on the skirt. The band may be used as an insert, placed above a ruffle, or used at the lower edge of the skirt.

The yoke seam and neck edge will be trimmed with entredeux and gathered lace (page 110). Make a strip of entredeux with gathered lace the length of all edges plus 6" (15 cm).

A slip of opaque batiste will prevent the undergarments from showing through. A ribbon rosette may be used as an accessory.

Beauty pins can be used to close an heirloom garment. The pins replace the buttons and buttonholes in fine, sheer fabrics that are not interfaced. Beauty pins may be gold-plated or hand-painted.

How to Make an Heirloom Dress

1) **Cut** front yoke from heirloom fabric; cut lining from dress fabric, if desired. Layer front yokes, wrong sides together. Place foldline of back yoke pattern on fold of dress fabric; cut two yokes. Join front and back yokes at shoulders, using French seams (page 81).

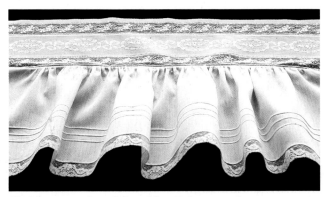

2) **Construct** band for skirt. Join entredeux to upper and lower edges of band. Cut ruffle according to pattern. Finish lower edge of ruffle with edging lace; gather upper edge as for puffing strip. Stitch ruffle to lower edge of band.

3) **Shorten** skirt pattern by width of band. Join skirt front and back at one seam. Complete placket. Join skirt and band. Stitch other side seam, matching seams of band and ruffle. Gather upper edge of skirt; join to yoke, step 3, page 81.

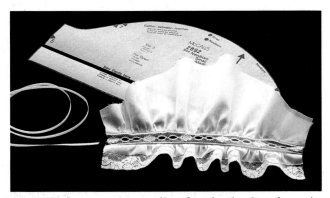

4) **Slash** sleeve pattern at line for elastic. Cut sleeve in two pieces; gather both edges of sleeve as for puffing strips. Cut beading 2" (5 cm) longer than circumference of arm; join to gathered edges of sleeve. Finish lower edge with flat lace. Set in sleeve. Insert ribbon in beading; tie bow.

5) **Join** entredeux to gathered lace; trim seam allowance of entredeux. Position entredeux on yoke next to seam, with end folded at placket edge as in step 7, right; zigzag to within 2" (5 cm) of corner. Fold trim under diagonally at corner.

6) **Fold** trim to miter corner at outer edge of lace so right side is up; place entredeux just above yoke seamline. The outer edge of the lace forms a right angle, and entredeux overlaps at inner corner. Miter other corners, and continue zigzagging trim to within 2" (5 cm) of placket.

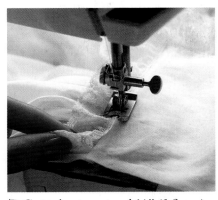

7) **Cut** trim to extend ½" (1.3 cm) beyond placket edge. Turn under ¼" (6 mm) twice so trim ends at placket edge; stitch. Attach entredeux with gathered lace to neck edge; finish ends as for yoke, above.

How to Make Heirloom Accessories

Rosettes. Cut 5 yards (4.6 m) of 1/16" (1.5 mm) or 1/8" (3 mm) double-faced satin ribbon. Mark every 2" (5 cm) or more; stop marks 12" to 15" (30.5 to 38 cm) from ends. Stitch through each mark using double thread; draw up tightly, and arrange loops. Knot thread. Hand-stitch rosette to garment.

Slip. Trim neck and armhole seam allowances to 1/4" (6 mm). Make placket at center back. Stitch both shoulder seams. Finish neck and armhole edges with entredeux joined to gathered lace (page 110); finish ends at placket as in step 7, page 113. Stitch side seams. Finish hem with flat lace (page 111).

How to Finish an Edge with French Binding

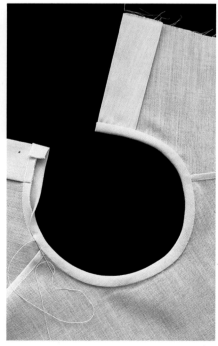

1) Cut 1¾" (4.5 cm) bias strip (page 101) of lightweight fabric 1" (2.5 cm) longer than edge. Press the strip in half lengthwise, wrong sides together.

2) Trim garment at seamline. Stitch binding to right side of garment, raw edges even, using 1/4" (6 mm) seam; wrap 1/2" (1.3 cm) of binding around ends to wrong side.

3) Fold binding in half over raw edges; press. Slipstitch folded edge of binding to previous stitching line.

How to Sew an Heirloom Bonnet

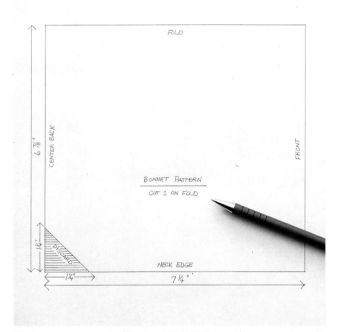

1) Draw rectangle 7¼" × 6⅞" (18.6 × 17.2 cm). Label long ends as neck edge and fold; label short sides as front and center back. Mark 1¼" (3.2 cm) on each side of center back and neck edge corner; connect dots with diagonal line for cutting line.

2) Join 15" (38 cm) lengths of fabric strips and trims (page 111) to 7¼" (18.6 cm) width. End with beading strip at back edge and gathered lace at front edge. Fold in half; position pattern on fabric. Cut bonnet. Stitch diagonal seam, using French seam (page 81).

3) Gather neck edge to 9" (23 cm). Finish with French binding, opposite. Cut 2 strips of ½" (1.3 cm) double-faced satin ribbon, each 24" (61 cm) long. Fold under ½" (1.3 cm) on one short end of each ribbon. Fold ribbon in half lengthwise; make running stitches, ¼" (6 mm) apart, on finished edges for 2" to 3" (5 to 7.5 cm).

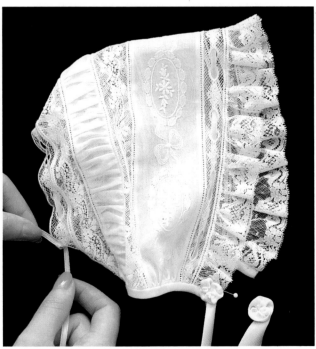

4) Pull thread to gather ribbon into circle. Secure end to ribbon, closing rosebud circle; hand-tack to bonnet at front edge of neck binding. Trim free ends of ribbons diagonally. Thread narrow ribbon through beading at center back; tighten and tie to finish.

Collars

Collars with trim are an easy and inexpensive way to dress up children's clothes, and are a practical and popular choice for adding special touches to classic styles. Collars may be edged with piping (**1**), lace (**2**), or both (**3**); they may be joined by fagoting to a bias strip (**4**) or to lace (**5**); or they may be machine-embroidered (**6**). See pages 118 to 121.

Fabrics such as lightweight batiste, broadcloth, calico, organdy, and voile are suitable for collars. Opaque fabrics minimize seam show-through. Crisp fabrics prevent curling of collar edges. Pipings and trims stabilize outer collar edges and eliminate the need for bulky, hard-to-handle interfacing in a small, curved collar.

Detachable Collars

Detachable collars permit a sewer to concentrate detail work on a small project. The collars can be worn with many garments or handed down to other children. Since the size of a child's neck changes slowly, a detachable collar may continue to be used as the child grows. Detachable collars may be finished with ties or hand-stitched to the inside of the neckline. Any of the collars on the following pages may be made as detachable collars, or stitched to the garment according to the pattern directions.

How to Make a Detachable Collar

1) Prepare collar. Staystitch neck edge of collar ⅛" (3 mm) from seamline; trim seam allowance on seamline. Apply French binding, steps 1 to 3, page 114.

2) Insert ½" (1.3 cm) of a 10" (25.5 cm) length of ¼" (6 mm) satin ribbon in each end of binding. Bar tack by zigzagging in place.

Alternative method. Prepare collar. Staystitch on collar seamline; trim seam allowance to ¼" (6 mm). Apply French binding, steps 1 to 3, page 114. Hand-stitch binding to inside of garment at neck edge.

Collars with Piping

Piping adds a tailored look to a collar, and may be used for a boy's or girl's collar. String or fine cord is an appropriate filler for piping in children's collars; preshrink the filler. Cut fabric strips for piping, page 101. Collars may also be trimmed with a combination of piping and lace, opposite.

How to Apply Piping to a Collar

1) **Cut** bias fabric strip 2" (5 cm) wide and length of outer edge of collar. Lay string or fine cord in center, and fold strip in half, wrong sides together. Stitch close to string, using zipper foot. Trim outer edge of collar and bias strip seam allowances to ¼" (6 mm).

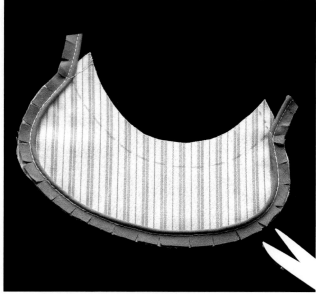

2) **Baste** piping to right side of upper collar, raw edges even. Clip seam allowance of piping at curves and neckline. Taper piping into seam allowance.

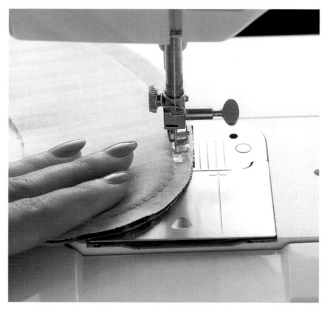

3) **Stitch** upper collar to undercollar on outer edge, with right sides together; stitch over basting line to join collars and piping.

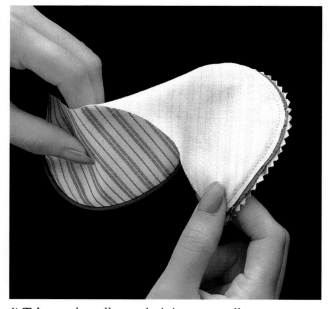

4) **Trim** undercollar and piping seam allowances to a scant ⅛" (3 mm). Trim upper collar seam allowance slightly with pinking shears; the upper collar seam allowance prevents piping seam allowance from showing through. Turn right side out. Press gently.

Collars with Lace Edging

Lace edging adds a feminine touch to a collar; it may be used alone or with piping (below). To keep the original size of a collar, reduce the width of the pattern by the width of the lace that is to be added at the edge. To make adding trims easier, adjust all seam allowances at the outer edge of the collar to ¼" (6 mm).

How to Apply Lace Edging to a Collar

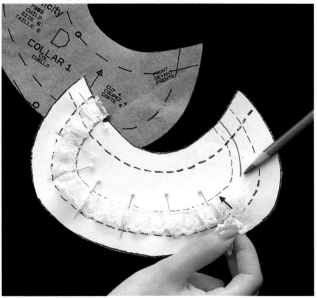

1) Trace collar pattern onto paper. Gather lace as in step 2, page 110; pin to pattern, with finished edge of lace at pattern seamline. Draw new seamline (arrow) at gathering line of lace. Draw new cutting line ¼" (6 mm) from new seamline. Cut collar, using adjusted pattern.

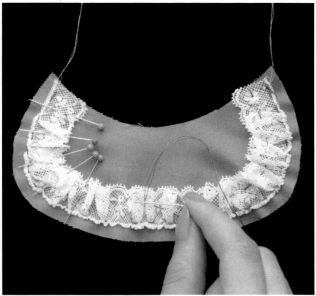

2) Baste lace to upper collar, right sides together, placing gathering line at new seamline. Adjust gathers so extra fullness is at curves. Baste ruffled portion of lace down to prevent catching in seam while stitching.

3) Stitch upper collar to undercollar on outer edge, right sides together, stitching over basting line to join collars and lace. Trim seam allowances as in step 4, opposite. Turn right side out. Remove basting. Press gently.

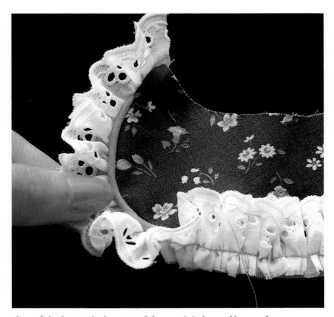

Combining piping and lace. Make adjusted pattern and cut collar as in step 1, above. Baste piping in place, step 2, opposite. Complete collar as in steps 2 and 3, above.

Collars with Fagoting

Fagoting is a method of joining two finished edges with an open, decorative stitch. The edges to be joined are basted to water-soluble stabilizer. Set the sewing machine for the fagoting stitch, or use a three-step zigzag stitch. Experiment with the stitches and make a test sample to determine the desired stitch width and length.

For a boy's collar, join a bias strip to the outer edge of the collar. For a girl's collar, join lace to the outer edge of the collar.

How to Make a Boy's or Girl's Collar with Fagoting

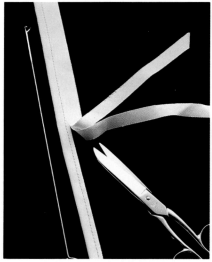

Boy's collar. 1) Cut 2" (5 cm) bias strip the length of the seamline at outer edge of collar. Fold right sides together. Stitch ¼" (6 mm) from fold, stretching fabric; trim to scant ⅛" (3 mm). Use loop turner to turn right side out.

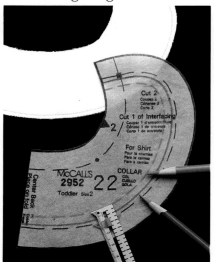

2) Decrease size of pattern at outer seamline by ⅜" (1 cm). Add ¼" (6 mm) seam allowance. Cut collar from adjusted pattern, and stitch upper collar to undercollar, using short stitch length; trim, turn, and press collar.

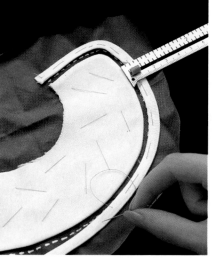

3) Baste collar to water-soluble stabilizer. Draw line ⅛" (3 mm) beyond outer edge. Press bias strip to follow curve of line, with seam on inner edge of curve. Baste bias strip to stabilizer at line.

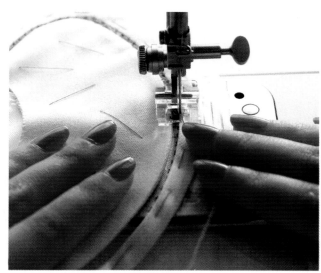

4) Center open area under presser foot. Stitch bias strip to collar, using fagoting stitch or 3-step zigzag stitch, *barely catching* the collar edge and bias strip alternately as you stitch. Remove stabilizer. Steam or spray with water, and blot with a towel; allow to dry.

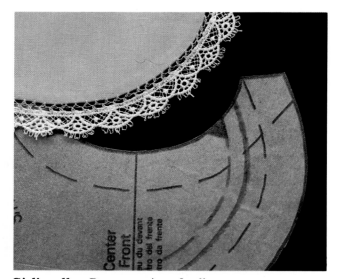

Girl's collar. Decrease size of collar pattern at outer seamline by width of lace plus ⅛" (3 mm). Add ¼" (6 mm) seam allowance. Cut and stitch collar as in step 2, above. Baste to water-soluble stabilizer. Draw line ⅛" (3 mm) from collar edge. Baste lace to stabilizer at line. Join lace to collar, using fagoting or 3-step zigzag stitch. Remove stabilizer as in step 4, left.

Collars with Machine Embroidery

Simplify the planning of stitch placement for machine-embroidered collars by choosing a collar pattern with rounded, rather than square, corners. Experiment with decorative stitches, and vary the stitch combinations. You may want to create different looks, using machine embroidery threads. Rayon thread produces a shinier finish than cotton thread.

For a sheer machine-embroidered collar, use silk organza or cotton organdy. When two layers of these fabrics are used, a shadow effect can be created by trimming away portions of one layer. Use appliqué scissors; the large, duckbill-shaped edge and angled handles allow you to trim close to the fabric without cutting into adjacent fabric.

How to Machine-embroider a Sheer Collar

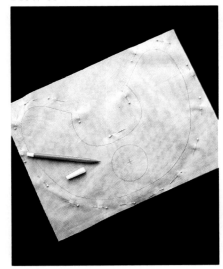  

1) Cut two layers of fabric 2" (5 cm) larger than the pattern; pin wrong sides together. Trace pattern, without seam allowances, onto fabric. Mark center of collar for placement of embroidery.

2) Embroider center design, using machine or hand stitches; outline with twin-needle stitching. Stitch decorative border pattern on outer edge; stitch additional row of stitching, if desired.

Shadow effect. Trim one layer of fabric from underside of collar; use appliqué scissors, with duckbill flat on fabric not being cut. Cut close to stitching. Trim outer edge close to stitching.

Especially for Boys

Boys' clothing usually ranges from traditional classic to well-worn sports clothes. However, some occasions call for special attire. Accessorize a boy's suit with suspenders, a bow tie, or a reversible vest.

Suspenders are quick and easy to make, using belting, or decorative elastic. Suspenders should be ⅛" (3 mm) narrower than the hardware.

There are two styles of suspenders: crisscross and cross-brace. Both styles require clips to fasten to the pants

waistband and adjusters for easy length alterations as the child grows.

To prevent suspenders from slipping off the shoulders, you may use a slide for crisscross suspenders or make a cross-brace to hold suspenders together in front.

To determine the finished length of crisscross suspenders, measure the child diagonally across the shoulder. For cross-brace suspenders, measure straight over the shoulder.

How to Make Crisscross Suspenders

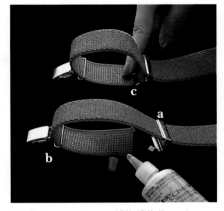

1) Cut two straps 10" (25.5 cm) longer than finished suspender length. Apply liquid fray preventer to cut ends. Insert one end through adjuster (**a**), then through clip (**b**), then back to adjuster; insert, and close tab (**c**).

2) Insert free ends through slide by bringing both ends of straps through side openings and out lower end of slide. Straps cross on back of slide.

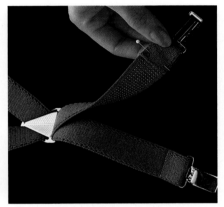

3) Thread free end through back clips; turn 1" (2.5 cm) to wrong side. Double-stitch through both thicknesses of strap. Position back slide and front adjusters for comfortable fit.

How to Make Cross-brace Suspenders

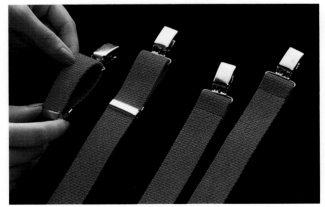

1) Cut two straps 10" (25.5 cm) longer than finished suspender length. Apply liquid fray preventer to cut ends. Attach adjusters and clips, as in steps 1 and 3, above.

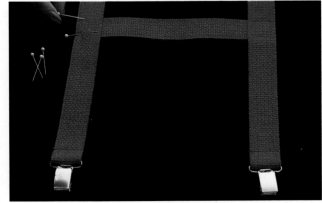

2) Try on suspenders with adjusters in back; position adjusters for comfortable fit. Cut cross-brace to fit at mid-chest between outer edges of straps. Apply liquid fray preventer to cut ends. Place cross-brace under straps; stitch as shown.

Reversible Vest with Bow Tie

A reversible vest may be coordinated with a bow tie and suspenders. For the vest, select two fabrics that are similar in weight and have the same care requirements. Interface the entire vest front for a crisp look and for support in the closure area. Gripper snaps, attached with a decorative prong for both the ball and socket, allow the vest to lap correctly when reversed.

For an easy-to-sew bow tie, cut fabric either on the bias or straight grain. Cut fabric for the bow 3½" × 9" (9 × 23 cm), for the knot 3" × 2" (7.5 × 5 cm), and for the neck band 2½" (6.5 cm) wide by the length of the neck measurement plus 1½" (3.8 cm). (Take neck measurement over the shirt.) For interfacing, cut a piece of polyester fleece, 1½" × 9" (3.8 × 23 cm). Attach hook and loop tape to the ends of the neck band for easier dressing. This size will be appropriate up to a Boys' size 10.

How to Make a Bow Tie

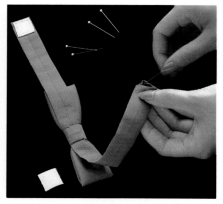

1) Fold all fabric strips lengthwise, with right sides together, and stitch with ¼" (6 mm) seam; press open. Turn the strips right side out; press flat, centering seam.

2) Insert fleece in strip for bow. Fold ends of strip to center back, overlapping ends ¼" (6 mm); stitch. Wrap center of bow tightly with double thread. Tack center back of bow to center of neck band.

3) Wrap strip for knot around bow and neck band, lapping ends; hand-stitch in place. On ends of neck band, turn in raw edges ¼" (6 mm). Stitch hook and loop tape to ends of neck band (page 84).

How to Make a Reversible Vest

 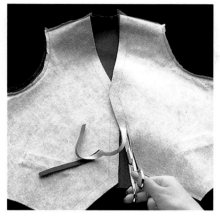 

1) Cut two fronts and one back from fabric; repeat, using coordinating fabric. Follow pattern directions to attach pockets to interfaced vest front. Stitch all shoulder seams; press open.

2) Stitch vests together at front, neck, and armhole edges, right sides together, matching shoulder seams. Trim seam allowances to ¼" (6 mm); clip curves to stitching. Press seams open.

3) Turn vest right side out by pulling front through shoulder to back, one side at a time. Press, positioning seamline exactly on the edge.

4) Stitch side seams of both layers in one continuous step, matching armhole seams. Press seams open. Trim seam allowances to ⅜" (1 cm).

5) Stitch lower raw edges, with right sides together and side seams matching; leave 3" (7.5 cm) opening for turning. Trim seam allowances to ¼" (6 mm); trim corners.

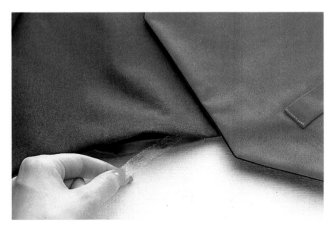 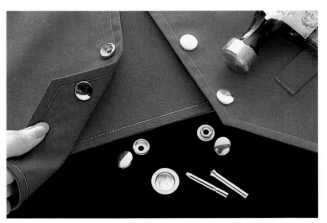

6) Turn vest right side out through opening at lower edge. Press lower edge, positioning seamline exactly on the edge. At opening, turn in raw edges, and fuse. Topstitch vest ¼" (6 mm) from edges, if desired.

7) Mark snap positions on both sides of each vest front. Apply snaps according to package directions, using decorative caps on both parts of snaps.

Index

Cy DeCosse Incorporated offers
fine sewing accessories to subscribers.
For information write:

Sewing Accessories
5900 Green Oak Drive
Minnetonka, MN 55343